The School Mathem

When the SMP was founded in 1961, its main objective was to devise radically new secondary school mathematics courses to reflect, more adequately than did the traditional syllabuses, the up-to-date nature and usages of mathematics. The first texts produced embodied new courses for O-level and A-level, and SMP GCE examinations were set up, available to schools through any of the GCE examining boards.

Since its beginning the SMP has continued to develop new materials and approaches to the teaching of mathematics. Further series of texts have been produced to meet new needs, and the original books are revised or replaced in the light of changing circumstances and experience in the classroom.

The SMP A-level course is now covered by *Revised Advanced Mathematics Books 1, 2* and *3*. Five shorter texts cover the material of the various sections of the A-level examination SMP Further Mathematics. The SMP Additional Mathematics syllabus has been revised and a new text replaces the original two books at this level.

The six Units of *SMP 7–13*, designed for pupils in that age-range, provide a course which is widely used in primary schools, middle schools and the first two years of secondary schools. A useful preliminary to Unit 1 of *SMP 7–13* is *Pointers*, a booklet for teachers which offers suggestions for mathematical activities with young children.

There is now a range of SMP materials for the eleven to sixteen age-range. The SMP O-level course is covered by *Books 1, 2* and *New Books 3, 4, 5*. *Books A–G* and *X, Y, Z*, together with the booklets of the *SMP Calculator Series*, also cover the O-level course, while *Books A–H* provide a CSE course for which most CSE boards offer a suitable examination.

SMP 11–16, designed to cater for about the top 85% of the ability range, is the newest SMP secondary school course, providing varied materials which facilitate the provision of a differentiated curriculum to match the varying abilities of pupils. Publication of this course began in 1983 and will be complete in 1988.

Teacher's Guides accompany all these series.

The SMP has produced many other texts, and teachers are encouraged to obtain each year from Cambridge University Press, The Edinburgh Building, Shaftesbury Road, Cambridge CB2 2RU, the full list of SMP publications currently available. In the same way, help and advice may always be sought by teachers from the Executive Director at the SMP Office, Westfield College, Kidderpore Avenue, London NW3 7ST. SMP syllabuses and other information may be obtained from the same address.

The SMP is continually evaluating old work and preparing for new. The effectiveness of the SMP's work depends, as it always has done, on the comments and reactions received from a wide variety of teachers – and also from pupils – using SMP materials. Readers of the texts can, therefore, send their comments to the SMP in the knowledge that they will be valued and carefully studied.

THE
SCHOOL
MATHEMATICS
PROJECT
New Book 3 : Part 1

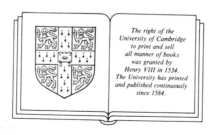

The right of the
University of Cambridge
to print and sell
all manner of books
was granted by
Henry VIII in 1534.
The University has printed
and published continuously
since 1584.

CAMBRIDGE UNIVERSITY PRESS

Cambridge

London   New York   New Rochelle

Melbourne   Sydney

Published by the Press Syndicate of the University of Cambridge
The Pitt Building, Trumpington Street, Cambridge CB2 1RP
32 East 57th Street, New York, NY 10022, USA
296 Beaconsfield Parade, Middle Park, Melbourne 3206, Australia

First published 1981
Reprinted 1982 (twice), 1983 (twice)

Printed in Great Britain at the
University Press, Cambridge

British Library cataloguing in publication data

School Mathematics Project
The School Mathematics Project
New Book 3
Part 1
1. Mathematics – 1961–
510   QA39.2
ISBN 0 521 28408 2

Contents

Preface

SMP Books 1–5 were published in the early sixties and have remained as the basic SMP O-level course, unchanged except for metrication. The revision of *Books 3, 4* and *5* draws on the experience of teaching with the original texts and incorporates other material developed by the SMP during the intervening years. While the mathematical content remains fundamentally unchanged the order of presentation of the material has been modified; the TEC Level I mathematics objectives have been borne in mind throughout the writing. The aim has been to make the texts accessible to a wider range of pupils, with clearer explanations and more carefully graded exercises, giving attention both to the practice of the necessary technical skills and to the use of the concepts in a variety of contexts. The electronic calculator is seen as the primary calculating aid throughout the books. Suggestions for ways in which pupils can use computers as an aid to learning mathematics are made at appropriate points in the latter half of the course. Each chapter concludes with a Summary exercise and a Miscellaneous exercise. Answers to about half the questions in exercises other than summary, miscellaneous and revision are provided at the end of each book; other answers are to be found in the accompanying *Teacher's Guides.*

The new books, like their predecessors, provide opportunities for the teacher to develop topics beyond the SMP O-level examination syllabuses, both of which are fully covered in the texts.

The 'two books per year' arrangement of the 'lettered' books has proved convenient and economical. It is hoped that presenting the last three years' work in five volumes rather than three will give schools the flexibility to allow for the different paces at which pupils work through the course. There is a range of SMP material designed for the first two years of the secondary school. Besides *Books 1* and *2, Books A—D, Cards I* and *II* and *Units 5* and *6* of *SMP 7–13* can be used. *SMP New Book 3* is written to follow from any of these alternatives; in addition it contains sufficient material for pupils who transfer to the SMP course at this stage.

The authors of the original books, on whose contributions this series is based, are named in *The School Mathematics Project: The First Ten Years,* published by Cambridge University Press.

SMP New Books 3, 4 and *5* have been produced by

David Cundy	Timothy Lewis
Giles Dickins	Charles Parker
Colin Goldsmith	Alan Tammadge
Katie Hairs	Nigel Webb
John Hersee	Lynette Weekley

and edited by David Cundy.

Many others have helped with advice and criticism, particularly the teachers and pupils who have tested the material in draft form.

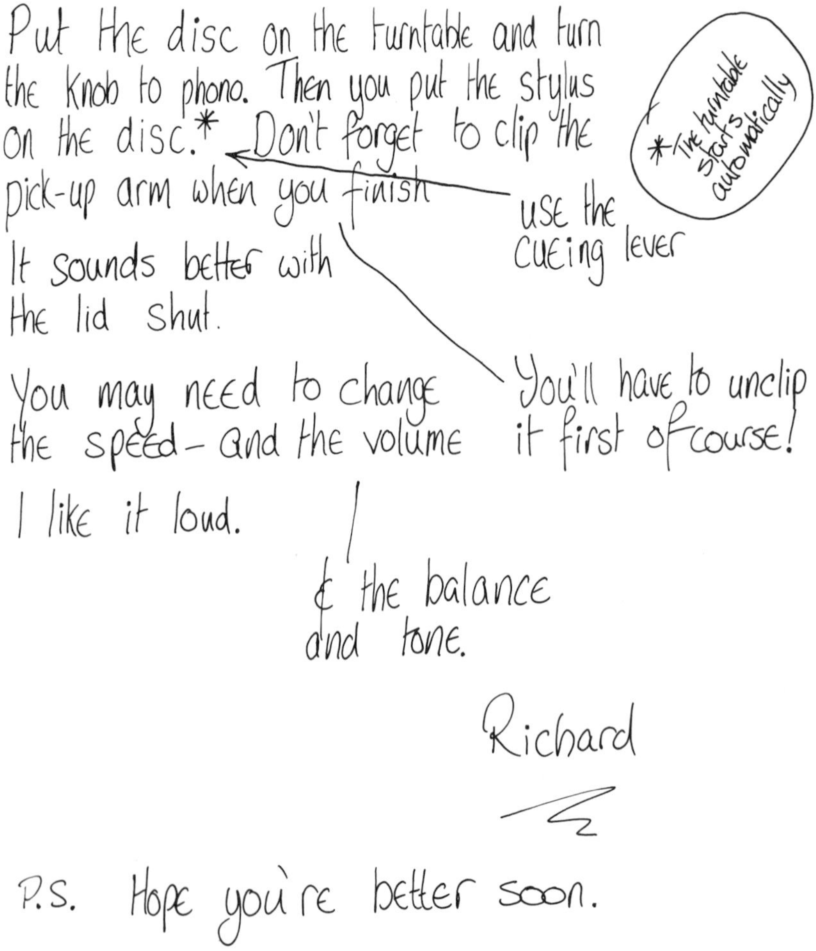

Put the disc on the turntable and turn the knob to phono. Then you put the stylus on the disc.* Don't forget to clip the pick-up arm when you finish ———— use the cueing lever

*The turntable starts automatically

It sounds better with the lid shut.

You may need to change the speed – and the volume

You'll have to unclip it first of course!

I like it loud.

& the balance and tone.

Richard

P.S. Hope you're better soon.

Figure 1

1

Flow charts and functions

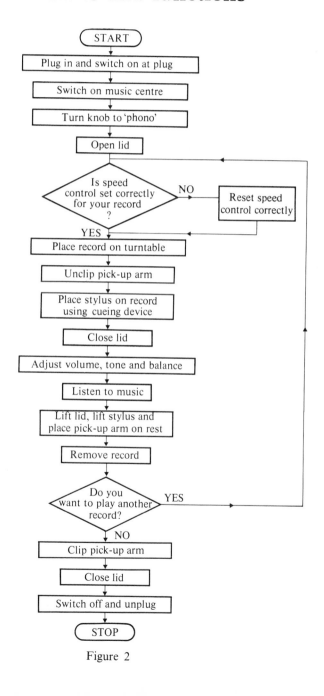

Figure 2

1. FLOW CHARTS

When John was ill Richard lent him his music centre so that he could play his records. Richard left a note explaining how to use it. (See Figure 1.) Richard's brother thought he would try to make things easier, so he made up a flow chart. (See Figure 2.)

Do you think the flow chart will help John to use Richard's music centre properly? How can things still go wrong?

'Flow charts' or 'flow diagrams' are used by businessmen, industrialists, scientists, geographers and others to describe an order in which things happen or to give instructions. The examples in this section are concerned with giving instructions. Notice that three types of box are used:

The 'running track', (   ) , is used for the beginning and end.

The 'diamond', ◇ , is used for 'decision boxes' containing questions

needing the answer 'Yes' or 'No'.

The 'rectangle', [   ] , is used for all other instructions.

It is conventional to start each flow chart with (START) and end it with

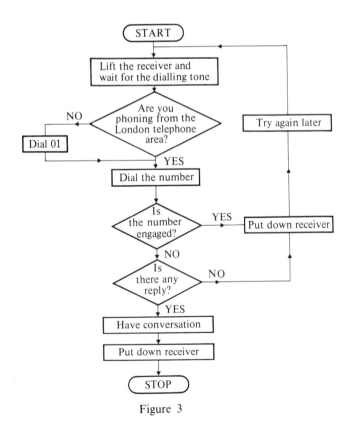

Figure 3

(STOP) . There is no need for you to write these in every time, nor to spend a long time ruling boxes.

Figure 3 is a flow chart showing how to make a telephone call to a number in London. Could the flow chart be improved? What happens, for example, if you get the continuous 'number unobtainable' tone?

In both Figure 2 and Figure 3 there are lines which leave a decision box and go back to an earlier instruction. These lines create loops in the charts; what effect do they have?

Exercise A

Draw flow charts to show someone how to do a few of the following:

1   cross a road;

2   ride a bicycle away from the kerb;

3   boil an egg;

4   bake a cake;

5   inflate a bicycle tyre;

6   look up the meaning of a word in a dictionary;

7   make a pot of tea.

2. FLOW CHARTS FOR ARITHMETIC

Flow charts can also be used for listing instructions where numbers are involved. It is helpful to write down the intermediate results, after each instruction, like this:

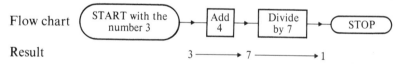

(Notice that the flow chart can be written across the page to save space.)

Exercise B

Follow through these flow charts, writing down the result at each stage, as in the example above.

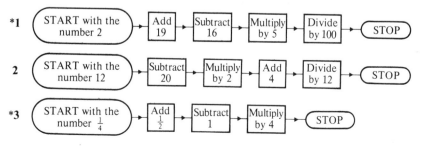

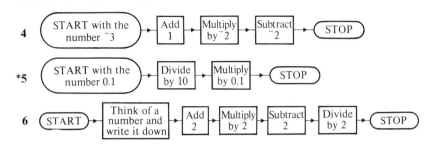

4

*5

6

Repeat this flow chart with several different numbers. What number would you start with to obtain 1000 as your final answer?

7

Repeat with several different numbers. What number or numbers can you start with to obtain zero as your final answer?

3. LETTERS FOR NUMBERS

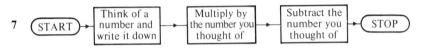

If you choose 5 as your number the instructions produce this result:

$$5 \longrightarrow 10 \longrightarrow 13$$

In general, if we write x for the number chosen, the result is:

$$x \longrightarrow 2x \longrightarrow 2x + 3$$

(Notice that we write $x \times 2$ as $2x$.)

The flow chart describes a method of changing x to $2x + 3$. We can write

$$f : x \longrightarrow 2x + 3$$

(which you can think of as 'the flow chart which changes x to $2x + 3$')

or $$f(x) = 2x + 3$$

('the result of putting x through the flow chart is $2x + 3$').

Since the result of putting 5 through the flow chart is 13, we can write $f(5) = 13$.

Compare the flow chart above with this one:

START → Think of a number → Add 3 → Multiply by 2 → STOP

Now the result is: $x \longrightarrow x + 3 \longrightarrow 2(x + 3)$

Notice the use of brackets in $2(x + 3)$, telling us to add 3 before multiplying by 2. Does this order of instructions give the same result as before if you choose 5

as your number? This flow chart changes x to $2(x + 3)$ so we can write
$f : x \longrightarrow 2(x + 3)$ or $f(x) = 2(x + 3)$.

Here are some more examples of describing what a flow chart does by using letters.

Flow chart   (START) → | Think of a number | → | Subtract 7 | → | Divide by 2 | → (STOP)

Result $q \longrightarrow q - 7 \longrightarrow \dfrac{q - 7}{2}$

Algebraic description $f : q \longrightarrow \dfrac{q - 7}{2}$ or $f(q) = \dfrac{q - 7}{2}$

Notice that it does not matter which letter is used. Also notice that $(q - 7) \div 2$ can be written in several ways:

$$\frac{q - 7}{2} \quad \text{or} \quad \tfrac{1}{2}(q - 7) \quad \text{or} \quad (q - 7)/2.$$

Can you see why these are all the same?
Check that if q is 19 the result of the flow chart is

$$19 \longrightarrow 12 \longrightarrow 6$$

or $f(19) = \dfrac{19 - 7}{2} = \dfrac{12}{2} = 6.$

Flow chart   (START) → | Think of a number | → | Divide by 2 | → | Subtract 7 | → (STOP)

Result $q \longrightarrow \dfrac{q}{2} \longrightarrow \dfrac{q}{2} - 7$

Algebraic description $g : q \longrightarrow \dfrac{q}{2} - 7$ or $g(q) = \dfrac{q}{2} - 7$

Notice again that it does not matter which letter is used as the flow chart letter although f, g or h are the most usual.
$\dfrac{q}{2} - 7$ can also be written as $\tfrac{1}{2}q - 7$. Can you see why?
Check that if q is 19 the result of the flow chart is

$$19 \longrightarrow 9\tfrac{1}{2} \longrightarrow 2\tfrac{1}{2}$$

or $g(19) = \dfrac{19}{2} - 7 = 9\tfrac{1}{2} - 7 = 2\tfrac{1}{2}.$

Exercise C

*1   Show the result of putting the letter x through each of the following flow charts and describe the flow chart in the form $f : x \longrightarrow \ldots$ and in the form $f(x) = \ldots$ Check your result by choosing a number to put through the flow chart and substituting the same number for x in $f(x)$.

(a)

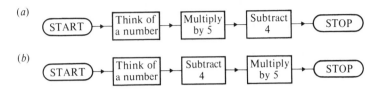

(b)

2 Repeat question 1 for the following flow charts.

(a)

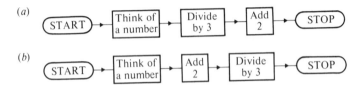

(b)

*3 (a) Give flow charts for (i) $f:x \longrightarrow 3x + 4$; (ii) $g:x \longrightarrow 3(x + 4)$.
  (b) For flow chart (i), check that $f(5) = 19$. What is the value of $f(2)$?
  (c) For flow chart (ii), check that $g(5) = 27$. What is the value of $g(2)$?

4 (a) Give flow charts for (i) $f:x \longrightarrow 7x - 5$; (ii) $g:x \longrightarrow 7(x - 5)$.
  (b) Use your flow charts to help you find the values of $f(6)$ and $g(6)$.

5 (a) Give flow charts for (i) $f:y \longrightarrow \frac{1}{2}y - 3$; (ii) $g:z \longrightarrow \frac{1}{2}(z - 3)$.
  (b) Use your flow charts to find the values of $f(10)$ and $g(10)$.

6 (a) Draw a flow chart for $f:t \longrightarrow \dfrac{t - 5}{3}$.

  (b) Draw a new flow chart which is the same as the one that you have just drawn except that the last two boxes before the STOP are in the opposite order. Describe this new flow chart in the form $f:t \longrightarrow \dots$

7 Give at least two different flow charts for $f:z \longrightarrow \dfrac{z + 3}{2}$.

One could contain the instruction | Halve the result |

Another should start with: 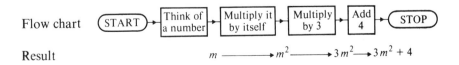

4. SQUARES, RECIPROCALS AND CHANGES OF SIGN

Squares

Flow chart   START → Think of a number → Multiply it by itself → Multiply by 3 → Add 4 → STOP

Result $m \longrightarrow m^2 \longrightarrow 3m^2 \longrightarrow 3m^2 + 4$

Algebraic description $\quad f : m \longrightarrow 3m^2 + 4 \quad$ or $\quad f(m) = 3m^2 + 4$

Notice that $m \times m$ is written m^2, and that $m^2 \times 3$ is written $3m^2$.
If the number we start with is 5 we finish with 79; $\quad 5 \to 25 \to 75 \to 79$
or $f(5) = 3 \times 5^2 + 4 = 3 \times 25 + 4 = 75 + 4 = 79$.

Flow chart $\quad$ (START) $\to$ | Think of a number | $\to$ | Multiply by 3 | $\to$ | Add 4 | $\to$ | Square the result (multiply it by itself) | $\to$ (STOP)

Result $\qquad\qquad\qquad\qquad m \longrightarrow 3m \longrightarrow 3m + 4 \longrightarrow (3m + 4)^2$

Algebraic description $\quad g : m \longrightarrow (3m + 4)^2 \quad$ or $\quad g(m) = (3m + 4)^2$

Notice the use of brackets, telling us to calculate $3m + 4$ before squaring.
If we start with 5 we finish with 361; $\quad 5 \longrightarrow 15 \longrightarrow 19 \longrightarrow 361$
or $\quad g(5) = (3 \times 5 + 4)^2 = (15 + 4)^2 = 19^2 = 361$.

Reciprocals

The reciprocal of a number is obtained by dividing 1 by the number. For example, the reciprocal of 2 is $1 \div 2$, i.e. $\frac{1}{2}$, and the reciprocal of 3 is $\frac{1}{3}$. What is the reciprocal of 4? What is the reciprocal of x?

The reciprocal of $\frac{3}{4}$ is $1 \div \frac{3}{4} = 1 \times \frac{4}{3} = \frac{4}{3}$. The reciprocal of $\frac{5}{6}$ is $\frac{6}{5}$. What is the reciprocal of $\frac{2}{3}$? What is the reciprocal of $\frac{x}{y}$?

The reciprocal of $\frac{1}{2}$ is $\frac{2}{1} = 2$.

What is the reciprocal of $\frac{1}{3}$? What is the reciprocal of $\frac{1}{x}$?

Flow chart $\quad$ (START) $\to$ | Think of a number | $\to$ | Find reciprocal | $\to$ | Multiply by 4 | $\to$ | Divide by 3 | $\to$ (STOP)

Result $\qquad\qquad\qquad\qquad z \longrightarrow \frac{1}{z} \longrightarrow \frac{4}{z} \longrightarrow \frac{4}{3z}$

Algebraic description $\quad f : z \longrightarrow \dfrac{4}{3z} \quad$ or $\quad f(z) = \dfrac{4}{3z}$

Notice that $\dfrac{1}{z} \times 4 = \dfrac{4}{z}$ and that $\dfrac{4}{z} \div 3 = \dfrac{4}{z} \times \dfrac{1}{3} = \dfrac{4 \times 1}{z \times 3} = \dfrac{4}{3z}$.

Starting with 7 we finish with $\dfrac{4}{21}$; $\quad 7 \longrightarrow \dfrac{1}{7} \longrightarrow \dfrac{4}{7} \longrightarrow \dfrac{4}{21}$

or $f(7) = \dfrac{4}{3 \times 7} = \dfrac{4}{21}$.

Changes of sign

Flow chart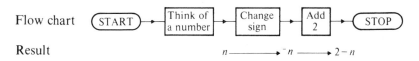

Result $\qquad n \longrightarrow {}^-n \longrightarrow 2-n$

Algebraic description $f : n \longrightarrow 2 - n$ or $f(n) = 2 - n$.

Notice that ${}^-n + 2 = 2 + {}^-n = 2 - n$.
Starting with 3 we finish with ${}^-1$; $3 \longrightarrow {}^-3 \longrightarrow {}^-1$ or $f(3) = 2 - 3 = {}^-1$.

Exercise D

*1   Find a simple algebraic description of these flow charts in the form $f(x) = \ldots$ Check by putting 2 through the flow chart and working out $f(2)$.

(a)

(b)

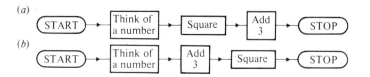

2   Repeat question 1 for the following flow charts:

(a)

(b)

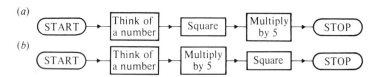

*3   Repeat question 1 for the following flow charts:

(a)

(b)

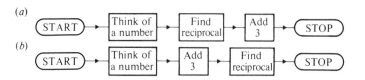

4   Repeat question 1 for the following flow charts:

(a)

(b)

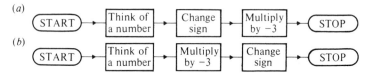

*5   (a) Give flow charts for (i) $f : t \longrightarrow \frac{1}{2}t^2$;   (ii) $g : t \longrightarrow (\frac{1}{2}t)^2$.
   (b) Use your flow charts to find $f(6)$ and $g(6)$.

6 (a) Give flow charts for

(i) $f:x \longrightarrow \dfrac{1}{2x}$;   (ii) $g:x \longrightarrow \dfrac{1}{x+2}$;   (iii) $h:x \longrightarrow \dfrac{3}{x+2}$.

(b) Find the values of $f(\tfrac{1}{2})$, $g(^-3)$ and $h(4)$.

*7 (a) Give flow charts for (i) $f:x \longrightarrow 3-x$; (ii) $g:x \longrightarrow 1-3x$.

(b) Find the value of x for which $f(x) = 0$.

(c) Find the value of x for which $g(x) = 0$.

8 (a) Give flow charts for

(i) $f:t \longrightarrow (t+3)^2$; (ii) $g:t \longrightarrow t^2+3$; (iii) $h:t \longrightarrow t^2+9$.

(b) Use your flow charts to find $f(2)$, $g(2)$ and $h(2)$.

(c) Can you find a value of t for which $f(t) = h(t)$?

*9 Give flow charts for

(a) $f:x \longrightarrow (3x+1)^2$;   (b) $g:x \longrightarrow 3x^2+1$;

(c) $f:x \longrightarrow 3-4x$;   (d) $g:x \longrightarrow 3+4x$.

10 Give flow charts for

(a) $f:x \longrightarrow \tfrac{1}{2}(3-x)$;   (b) $g:x \longrightarrow \dfrac{1}{2-x}$;

(c) $f:x \longrightarrow \dfrac{1}{x}+\dfrac{1}{2}$;   (d) $g:x \longrightarrow 1-\dfrac{1}{x}$.

*11 (a) For the flow chart

find $f(2)$ and $f(\tfrac{2}{3})$.

(b) Describe the flow chart algebraically in the form $f:x \longrightarrow \ldots$ and in the form $f(x) = \ldots$

12 (a) For the flow chart

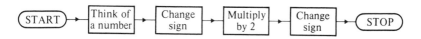

find $f(1)$, $f(3)$ and $f(\tfrac{1}{2})$.

(b) Give a simpler flow chart which has the same effect.

5. FUNCTIONS

If we want to put g : $x \longrightarrow 2x+3$
into words we can say   'the *function* g such that x *maps onto* $2x+3$'.
             $g(x)$ $= 2x+3$ can be read as
'the *image* of x under the function g is $2x+3$'.

Example 1

Find a function such that 2 maps onto 6, 3 maps onto 9 and 4 maps onto 12.

One possible way to do this is to multiply by three, so a possible function is $f:x \longrightarrow 3x$.

Example 2

Find the image of 2 under the function $f : x \longrightarrow 3 - 5x$.

$f(2) = 3 - 5 \times 2 = 3 - 10 = {}^-7$; the image is ${}^-7$.

Exercise E

*1   Find the images of ${}^-1$, 0, and 1 under $f : x \longrightarrow 2 - 3x$.

2   Find the images of ${}^-1$, 0, 1 and 2 under $g : x \longrightarrow (x - 1)^2$.

*3   Find the images of ${}^-1$, 1 and 2 under $h : x \longrightarrow \dfrac{1}{3x} + \dfrac{1}{3}$.

4   Find the images of 1, 0.4 and 0.3 under $f : t \longrightarrow \dfrac{10}{8 - 10t}$.

*5   Find a function such that 4 maps onto 7, 5 maps onto 8 and 6 maps onto 9.

6   Find a function such that 4 maps onto 7, 5 maps onto 9 and 6 maps onto 11.

*7   Find a function such that 4 maps onto 6, 5 maps onto 5 and 6 maps onto 4.

8   Find a function such that 3 maps onto 0, 4 maps onto ${}^-1$ and 5 maps onto ${}^-2$.

*9   Find a function such that 2 maps onto 4, 3 maps onto 9 and 4 maps onto 16.

10   Find a function such that 3 maps onto 16, 4 maps onto 25 and 5 maps onto 36.

6. FLOW CHARTS AND SEQUENCES

The flow chart in Figure 4 gives instructions for writing down the first ten terms of a sequence of numbers.

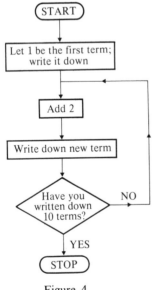

For this sequence,
the first term is 1;
the second term is   first term $+ 2 = 3$,
the third term is   second term $+ 2 = 5$,
the fourth term is   third term $+ 2 = 7$
and so on.
We can write 'fourth term' as 'term$_4$' or, for short, t_4.
So for this sequence we have:

$t_1 = 1$

$t_2 = t_1 + 2 = 1 + 2 = 3$

$t_3 = t_2 + 2 = 3 + 2 = 5$

$t_4 = t_3 + 2 = 5 + 2 = 7$, etc.

Figure 4

What is t_6?   What is t_8?   If $t_n = 23$, what is n?

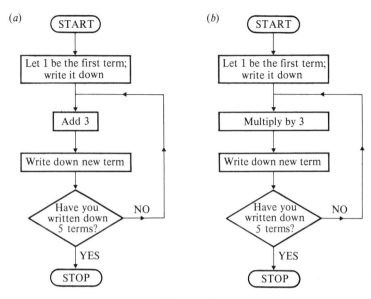

Figure 5

Exercise F

*1 For each of the flow charts in Figure 5, write down the terms of the sequence which it gives.

2 'The first term is 3; the next term is 4 more than the previous term.' Write down the first five terms of the sequence described. Draw a flow chart like those in question 1 to describe the sequence.

*3 Draw a flow chart to describe how to write down the first eight terms of the sequence which starts:

$$1000, \ 100, \ 10, \ 1, \ 0.1, \ \ldots$$

Write down the sixth term, t_6. What is t_8?

4 Copy and complete the table below for the sequences given by the flow charts in Figure 6.

	t_1	t_2	t_3	t_4	t_5	t_6	t_7	t_8	t_9	t_{10}
(a)	7			28						70
(b)				32						-53
(c)						10				1.25
(d)										

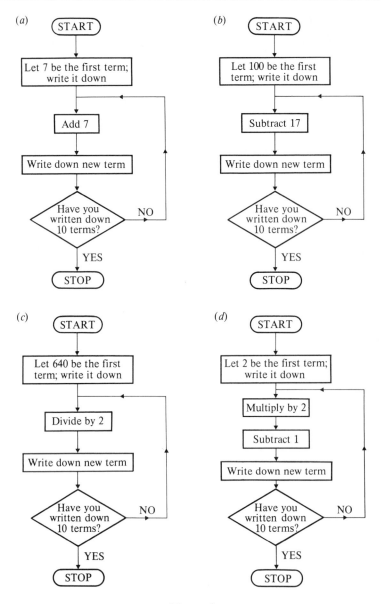

Figure 6

SUMMARY

Flow charts are used to give instructions or to describe an order of events.

Functions may be represented in flow chart form. For example, the following are various equivalent ways of describing a function which maps 2 onto 14, 3 onto 16, 4 onto 18, etc.

$f : x \longrightarrow 2(x + 5)$ the function f which maps x onto $2(x + 5)$
$f(x) = 2(x + 5)$ the image of x under the function f is $2(x + 5)$
and, for example, $f(3) = 16$.

$x \times 2$ is written $2x$. $x \times x$ is written x^2. The brackets in $2(x + 5)$ indicate that 5 must be added to x before multiplying by 2.

The reciprocal of x is $\dfrac{1}{x}$;   the reciprocal of $\dfrac{a}{b}$ is $\dfrac{b}{a}$.

Flow charts can be used to describe how to write down sequences. A useful shorthand for describing terms of a sequence is to call the first term t_1, the second term t_2, the third term t_3 and so on.

Summary exercise

1   Give the functions, in the form $f : x \longrightarrow \ldots$, for each of the following flow charts:

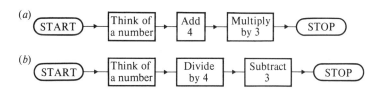

2   Give flow charts for these functions:

(a) $f : x \longrightarrow 2x - 5$;   (b) $g : x \longrightarrow 2(x - 5)$;   (c) $h : x \longrightarrow \dfrac{5}{x} - 2$;

(d) $f : x \longrightarrow \tfrac{1}{2}x - 5$;   (e) $g : x \longrightarrow \dfrac{x - 5}{2}$;   (f) $h : x \longrightarrow \dfrac{5}{x - 2}$.

3   For each of the functions in question 2 find the value of $f(1)$.

4   Write down the sequences produced by the flow charts in Figure 7. For each sequence draw a flow chart containing a shorter list of instructions which has the same effect.

5   Draw flow charts to describe how to obtain the first 10 terms of each of the sequences below. In each case give the values of t_6 and t_7.
   (a)   6, 12, 18, 24, 30, ...
   (b)   50, 47, 44, 41, 38, ...
   (c)   19, 37, 55, 73, 91, ...

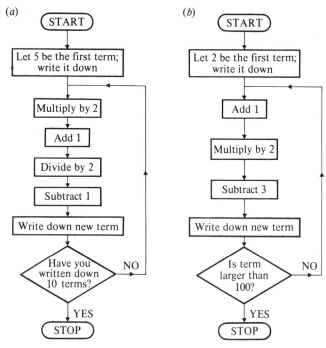

Figure 7

Miscellaneous exercise

1   Draw a flow diagram to show someone either (*a*) how to start a car or (*b*) how to make a dress.

2   In a knitting pattern for a pullover the instructions for knitting part of the rib start as follows:
'Using 3mm (no. 10) needles cast on 65 sts.
1st row: Sl.1, K.1, *P.1, K.1, repeat from * to the last stitch, K.1.
2nd row: Sl.1, *P.1, K.1, repeat from * to end of row.'
Draw a flow chart for this part of the knitting pattern.

3   Draw a flow chart for $f : x \longrightarrow 5 - \dfrac{6}{2 - 3x^2}$.   What is the value of $f(\frac{1}{2})$?

4   Find a function such that 2 maps onto 7,   3 maps onto 17 and 4 maps onto 31.

5   Find a function such that 3 maps onto $\frac{1}{2}$,   2 maps onto 1 and 4 maps onto $\frac{1}{3}$.

6   Find a function such that 3 maps onto $\frac{1}{2}$,   5 maps onto $\frac{1}{3}$ and 7 maps onto $\frac{1}{4}$.

7   Draw a flow chart to obtain the first ten terms of the sequence which starts
1, 1, 2, 3, 5, 8, 13, 21, ...

REVISION EXERCISE 1

1 Calculate:

    (a) $2\frac{1}{2} \times 1\frac{1}{2}$ (b) $\frac{1}{2} + \frac{1}{3} + \frac{1}{4}$ (c) $3\frac{1}{2} \div 2\frac{1}{3}$ (d) $\frac{3}{4} - \frac{2}{3}$

2 Write down the first ten prime numbers and calculate their mean. (1 is not a prime number.)

3 Calculate:

    (a) 0.2×0.3 (b) 0.11^2 (c) $150 \div 0.5$ (d) $375 \div 0.25$

4 Work out the marked angles in the diagrams in Figure 1. In (b) $PQ = QR$; in (c) AB is parallel to DCE.

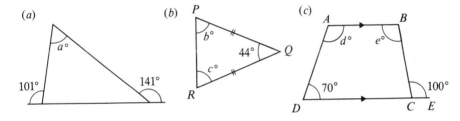

5 Calculate:

    (a) $(6 - 2) - (1 - 5)$ (b) $(^-3)^3$ (c) $\dfrac{3 - 8}{3 - 13}$ (d) $(1 - 4) \times (2 - 7)$

2

Standard form

1. POWERS OF TEN

When Sir Isaac Newton made his estimates of the mass of the sun, he gave the result

22 000 000 000 000 000 000 000 000 000 pounds.

To an accuracy of one significant figure, the mass of an electron is

0.000 000 000 000 000 000 000 000 000 9g.

It is not very convenient to have to write so many zeros when we wish to describe a very large or a very small quantity. Also, it is quite easy to make mistakes in arithmetic with such numbers by missing out zeros, or putting in extra ones, through losing count of them. We need a shorthand.

The sequence 1, 10, 100, 1000, 10 000, ... may be obtained by multiplying again and again by 10.

Figure 1

So	1,	10,	100,	1000,	10 000,	100 000
are	1,	10,	10×10,	$10 \times 10 \times 10$,	$10 \times 10 \times 10 \times 10$,	$10 \times 10 \times 10 \times 10 \times 10$
or	1,	10,	10^2,	10^3,	10^4,	10^5

When we write 10^5 for $10 \times 10 \times 10 \times 10 \times 10$, we call it 'ten to the power of five' and five is known as the index (plural: indices).

Notice that

$$10^3 \times 10^2 = 10 \times 10 \times 10 \times 10 \times 10 = 10^5$$

or, more briefly, $10^3 \times 10^2 = 10^{3+2} = 10^5$.

16

Compare these two versions of the same arithmetic:

Full version $1\,000\,000 \times 10\,000 = 10\,000\,000\,000$

Shorthand $10^6 \times 10^4 = 10^{6+4} = 10^{10}$

In general, $10^a \times 10^b = 10^{a+b}$

Notice now that

$$10^6 \div 10^4 = \frac{10 \times 10 \times 10 \times 10 \times 10 \times 10}{10 \times 10 \times 10 \times 10}$$

$$= 10 \times 10 = 10^2$$

or, more briefly, $10^6 \div 10^4 = 10^{6-4} = 10^2$.

In general, $10^a \div 10^b = 10^{a-b}$.

Now notice that this would require that

$$10^3 \div 10^3 = 10^{3-3} = 10^0.$$

But $10^3 \div 10^3 = 1000 \div 1000 = 1$

so if we are to be consistent we shall have to define 10^0 to be equal to 1. (This would correspond to going round the loop in Figure 1 zero times.)

We shall also require

$$10^2 \div 10^5 = 10^{2-5} = 10^{-3}.$$

But $10^2 \div 10^5 = \dfrac{10 \times 10}{10 \times 10 \times 10 \times 10 \times 10} = \dfrac{1}{10 \times 10 \times 10} = \dfrac{1}{10^3}$

so we ought to define $10^{-3} = \dfrac{1}{10^3}$. Similarly $10^{-2} = \dfrac{1}{10^2}$ and, in general,

$10^{-a} = \dfrac{1}{10^a}$.

The pattern is shown in the following table:

$$
\begin{array}{rcl}
10^5 & = & 100\,000 \\
10^4 & = & 10\,000 \\
10^3 & = & 1000 \\
10^2 & = & 100 \\
10^1 & = & 10 \\
10^0 & = & 1 \\
10^{-1} = \dfrac{1}{10^1} = \dfrac{1}{10} & = & 0.1 \\
10^{-2} = \dfrac{1}{10^2} = \dfrac{1}{100} & = & 0.01 \\
10^{-3} = \dfrac{1}{10^3} = \dfrac{1}{1000} & = & 0.001 \\
10^{-4} = \dfrac{1}{10^4} = \dfrac{1}{10\,000} & = & 0.0001
\end{array}
$$

Example 1

Simplify:

(a) $10^5 \times 10^{-2}$; (b) $10^{-3} \div 10^{-2}$.

(a) $10^5 \times 10^{-2} = 10^{5 + -2} = 10^3$

Check: $10^5 \times 10^{-2} = 10^5 \times \dfrac{1}{10^2} = \dfrac{100\,000}{100} = 1000 = 10^3$

(b) $10^{-3} \div 10^{-2} = 10^{-3 - -2} = 10^{-1} = \dfrac{1}{10}$

Check: $10^{-3} \div 10^{-2} = \dfrac{1}{1000} \div \dfrac{1}{100} = \dfrac{1}{1000} \times \dfrac{100}{1} = \dfrac{1}{10}$

Exercise A

*1 Simplify the following, leaving your answers as powers of ten:

(a) $10^5 \times 10^3$ (b) $10^4 \times 10^3$ (c) $10^5 \times 10^{-3}$ (d) $10^{-2} \times 10^6$
(e) $10^{-5} \times 10^3$ (f) $10^2 \times 10^{-6}$ (g) $10^{-2} \times 10^{-3}$ (h) $10^{-4} \times 10^{-5}$.

*2 Simplify the following, leaving your answers as powers of ten:

(a) $10^5 \div 10^3$ (b) $10^4 \div 10^3$ (c) $10^3 \div 10^7$ (d) $10^4 \div 10^6$
(e) $10^{-5} \div 10^{-7}$ (f) $10^{-4} \div 10^{-1}$ (g) $10^{-5} \div 10^{-2}$ (h) $10^{-2} \div 10^3$

3 State whether each of the following statements is true or false. Give a correct version of those which are false.

(a) $10^5 \times 10^4 = 10^{20}$ (b) $10^3 \times 10^5 = 10^5 \times 10^3$ (c) $10^8 \div 10^4 = 10^2$
(d) $10^8 \div 10^4 = 10^4 \div 10^8$ (e) $10^2 \times 10^2 = 100^2$ (f) $10^3 \times 10^2 = 100^5$
(g) $10^{-3} = 0.0001$ (h) $10^{-4} > 10^{-3}$

4 Simplify the following, leaving your answers as powers of ten:

(a) $\dfrac{10^5 \times 10^4}{10^3}$ (b) $\dfrac{10^{20}}{10^{10} \times 10^{10}}$ (c) $\dfrac{10^4 \times 10^{-3}}{10^2}$

(d) $\dfrac{10^{-4} \times 10^{-3}}{10^{-2}}$ (e) $\dfrac{10^{-2}}{0.1}$ (f) $\dfrac{10^2 \times 0.0001}{10\,000}$

2. STANDARD FORM

We have seen that $10\,000$ can be written as 10^4.

Because $20\,000 = 2 \times 10\,000$, we can write $20\,000$ as 2×10^4.
Similarly $21\,000 = 2.1 \times 10\,000 = 2.1 \times 10^4$.
Check: $21\,000 = 2100 \times 10$
$$= 210 \times 10^2$$
$$= 21 \times 10^3$$
$$= 2.1 \times 10^4$$

or, more briefly, $2\overrightarrow{1}\,\overrightarrow{0}\,\overrightarrow{0}\,0 = 2.1 \times 10^4$
(where each arrow indicates a factor of 10 : the 2 has to be moved four places to the right to bring it to the units place).

Also $\dfrac{1}{1000} = 10^{-3}$

so $0.005 = \dfrac{5}{1000} = 5 \times \dfrac{1}{1000} = 5 \times 10^{-3}$

and $0.0052 = \dfrac{5.2}{1000} = 5.2 \times \dfrac{1}{10^3} = 5.2 \times 10^{-3}.$

Check: $0.0052 = 0.052 \times \dfrac{1}{10}$

$= 0.52 \times \dfrac{1}{10^2}$

$= 5.2 \ \ \times \dfrac{1}{10^3}$

$= 5.2 \times 10^{-3}$

or, more briefly, $0.\overleftarrow{0}\,\overleftarrow{0}\,\overleftarrow{5}\,2 = 5.2 \times 10^{-3}$
(where each arrow indicates a factor of 10 : the 5 has to be moved three places to the left to bring it to the units place).

A number written in the form $A \times 10^n$, where n is an integer and $1 \leqslant A < 10$ (i.e. A is 1 or more, but less than 10), is said to be in 'standard form', 'standard index form' or 'scientific notation'. Here are some further examples.

Example 2

(a) $30\,000\,000 = 3 \times 10\,000\,000 = 3 \times 10^7$ $[3\,\overrightarrow{0}\,\overrightarrow{0}\,\overrightarrow{0}\,\overrightarrow{0}\,\overrightarrow{0}\,\overrightarrow{0}\,\overrightarrow{0}]$

(b) $0.000\,007 = \dfrac{7}{1000\,000} = 7 \times \dfrac{1}{10^6} = 7 \times 10^{-6}$ $[\overleftarrow{0}.\overleftarrow{0}\,\overleftarrow{0}\,\overleftarrow{0}\,\overleftarrow{0}\,\overleftarrow{0}\,7]$

(c) $2971.3 = 2.9713 \times 1000 = 2.9713 \times 10^3$ $[2\,\overrightarrow{9}\,\overrightarrow{7}\,\overrightarrow{1}.3]$

(d) $0.01234 = \dfrac{1.234}{100} = 1.234 \times \dfrac{1}{100} = 1.234 \times 10^{-2}$

(e) $300.01 = 3.0001 \times 10^2$

(f) $0.009\,09 = 9.09 \times 10^{-3}$

Exercise B

*1 Write each of the following numbers in standard form:
    (a) $800\,000$ (b) $0.000\,09$ (c) $48\,200$ (d) 0.0168

2 Write each of the following numbers in standard form:
    (a) 3100 (b) $0.000\,011$ (c) 234.5 (d) 0.0702

*3 Write each of the following numbers in full, not in standard form:
    (a) 2.8×10^3 (b) 5×10^{-4} (c) 7.98×10^5 (d) 6.01×10^{-2}

4 Write each of the following numbers in full, not in standard form:
    (a) 3.1×10^4 (b) 3.129×10^{-3} (c) 8.001×10^6 (d) 3.1×10^1

*5 Write the following scientific data in standard form:
    (a) the distance from the earth to the sun $= 150\,000\,000$ km;
    (b) the mass of the sun $= 2\,000\,000\,000\,000\,000\,000\,000\,000\,000\,000$ tonne;

(c) the velocity of light $= 299\,000\,000$ m/s;

(d) the mass of an electron $= 0.000\,000\,000\,000\,000\,000\,000\,000\,000\,9$ g.

6 Write the following scientific data in standard form:

(a) the velocity of α-radiation $= 20\,000\,000$ m/s;

(b) the wavelength of γ-radiation $= 0.000\,000\,000\,01$ m;

(c) the half-life of Uranium U-238 $= 4\,500\,000\,000$ years;

(d) the half-life of Polonium 214 $= 0.000\,16$ s.

3. UNITS

Standard form can be useful when changing from one unit to another in the metric system. The most common prefixes are kilo-, meaning 1000, and milli-, meaning $\dfrac{1}{1000}$.

For example, 1 km $= 1000$ m $= 10^3$ m

and 1 mg $= \dfrac{1}{1000}$ g $= 10^{-3}$ g.

So 43 km $= 43 \times 10^3$ m $= 4.3 \times 10^1 \times 10^3$ m $= 4.3 \times 10^4$ m

0.3 km $= 0.3 \times 10^3$ m $= 3 \times 10^{-1} \times 10^3$ m $= 3 \times 10^2$ m

43 mg $= 43 \times 10^{-3}$ g $= 4.3 \times 10^1 \times 10^{-3}$ g $= 4.3 \times 10^{-2}$ g.

Exercise C

Lengths

*1 Write the following lengths in standard form in metres:

(a) 5.7 km;   (b) 32 km;   (c) 0.87 km;   (d) 4 mm;   (e) 47 mm;   (f) 990 mm.

*2 There are 100 centimetres in 1 metre. Write the following lengths in standard form in metres:

(a) 1 cm;   (b) 1.9 cm;   (c) 23 cm;   (d) 0.7 cm;   (e) 363 cm;   (f) 0.087 cm.

3 Write the lengths given in question 2 in standard form in millimetres.

Masses

*4 Write the following masses in standard form in kilograms:

(a) 1 g;   (b) 5.8 g;   (c) 31.7 g;   (d) 1 mg;   (e) 39 mg;   (f) 476 mg.

*5 There are 1000 kg in 1 tonne. Write the following masses in standard form in kilograms:

(a) 1 tonne;   (b) 96 tonne;   (c) 250 tonne;   (d) 0.003 tonne.

Areas

*6 (a) How many square metres (m^2) are there in 1 km^2?

(b) Write the following areas in standard form in square metres:

(i) 4 km^2;   (ii) 0.3 km^2;   (iii) 56 cm^2;   (iv) 4970 mm^2.

*7 There are $10\,000$ m^2 in 1 hectare (1 ha).

(a) Write the following areas in standard form in square metres:

(i) 5 ha; (ii) 40 ha; (iii) 0.3 ha; (iv) 0.07 ha.

(b) Write the following areas in standard form in hectares:

(i) 1 m^2; (ii) 2000 m^2; (iii) 1 km^2; (iv) 0.7 km^2.

Volumes

*8 Volumes of fluids can be measured in litres (l). A litre is defined to be equivalent to a cubic decimetre (1 dm^3; a decimetre is $\frac{1}{10}$ m).

$1\ 1 = 1$ dm$^3 = \frac{1}{10} \times \frac{1}{10} \times \frac{1}{10}$ m$^3 = 10^{-3}$ m^3.

(a) Write the following volumes in standard form in cubic metres:

(i) 5 l; (ii) 0.15 l; (iii) 1 cm^3; (iv) 100 cm^3.

(b) Write the following volumes in standard form in litres:

(i) 1 m^3; (ii) 0.3 m^3; (iii) 1 cm^3; (iv) 1000 cm^3.

(c) Write the following volumes in standard form in cubic centimetres:

(i) 1 l; (ii) 0.4 l; (iii) 4 m^3; (iv) 5 mm^3.

9 (a) A milk-bottle contains 568 ml. (A millilitre is $\frac{1}{1000}$ litre.) Express the capacity in

(i) litres; (ii) cubic metres; (iii) cubic centimetres.

(b) A wine-bottle contains 75 cl. (A centilitre is $\frac{1}{100}$ litre.) Express the capacity in

(i) litres; (ii) cubic metres; (iii) cubic centimetres.

10 1 cm^3 of a particular liquid has a mass of 1 g. What would be the mass (in tonnes) of 1 m^3 of the liquid?

4. CALCULATIONS IN STANDARD FORM

Example 3

Calculate the following, giving the answers in standard form:

(a) $2 \times 10^3 \times 4 \times 10^2$ (b) $4 \times 10^5 \times 3 \times 10^6$ (c) $5.1 \times 10^{-3} \times 3 \times 10^{-2}$

(a) $2 \times 10^3 \times 4 \times 10^2 = 2 \times 10 \times 10 \times 10 \times 4 \times 10 \times 10$
$$= 2 \times 4 \times 10 \times 10 \times 10 \times 10 \times 10 = 8 \times 10^5$$

or, more briefly,

$2 \times 10^3 \times 4 \times 10^2 = 2 \times 4 \times 10^{3+2} = 8 \times 10^5$.

(b) $4 \times 10^5 \times 3 \times 10^6 = 4 \times 3 \times 10^{5+6} = 12 \times 10^{11}$
$$= 1.2 \times 10^1 \times 10^{11} = 1.2 \times 10^{12}$$

(Notice that 12×10^{11} is not in standard form.)

(c) $5.1 \times 10^{-3} \times 3 \times 10^{-2} = 5.1 \times 3 \times 10^{-3+-2} = 15.3 \times 10^{-5}$
$$= 1.53 \times 10^1 \times 10^{-5} = 1.53 \times 10^{-4}$$

Example 4

Calculate the following, giving the answers in standard form:

(a) $(6 \times 10^5) \div (3 \times 10^2)$ (b) $(3 \times 10^5) \div (6 \times 10^2)$

(a) $\dfrac{6 \times 10^5}{3 \times 10^2} = \dfrac{6 \times 10 \times 10 \times 10 \times 10 \times 10}{3 \times 10 \times 10} = \dfrac{6 \times 10 \times 10 \times 10}{3}$

$$= 2 \times 10 \times 10 \times 10 = 2 \times 10^3$$

or, more briefly,

$$(6 \times 10^5) \div (3 \times 10^2) = \frac{6}{3} \times 10^{5-2} = 2 \times 10^3.$$

(b) *Either* $(3 \times 10^5) \div (6 \times 10^2) = \frac{3}{6} \times 10^{5-2} = 0.5 \times 10^3 = 5 \times 10^{-1} \times 10^3$

$$= 5 \times 10^2$$

or $\dfrac{3 \times 10^5}{6 \times 10^2} = \dfrac{30 \times 10^4}{6 \times 10^2} = 5 \times 10^{4-2} = 5 \times 10^2.$

Exercise D

Calculate the following, leaving your answers in standard form:

*1	$2 \times 10^4 \times 3 \times 10^3$	2	$1.5 \times 10^5 \times 4 \times 10^2$
*3	$2.5 \times 10^6 \times 2 \times 10^{-2}$	4	$6 \times 10^{-4} \times 1.5 \times 10^7$
*5	$5 \times 10^7 \times 4 \times 10^3$	6	$3 \times 10^2 \times 6 \times 10^3$
*7	$8 \times 10^6 \times 6 \times 10^{-4}$	8	$2 \times 10^{-3} \times 4 \times 10^{-2}$
*9	$6 \times 10^{-3} \times 5 \times 10^{-2}$	10	$7 \times 10^2 \times 6 \times 10^{-5}$
*11	$8 \times 10^6 \div (2 \times 10^4)$	12	$6 \times 10^4 \div (3 \times 10^8)$
*13	$5 \times 10^5 \div (2 \times 10^2)$	14	$6 \times 10^6 \div (5 \times 10^3)$
*15	$8 \times 10^{-4} \div (2 \times 10^3)$	16	$6 \times 10^{-4} \div (2 \times 10^{-2})$
*17	$3 \times 10^4 \div (6 \times 10^2)$	18	$2 \times 10^7 \div (5 \times 10^3)$
*19	$3 \times 10^{-2} \div (4 \times 10^4)$	20	$2.4 \times 10^3 \div (5 \times 10^5)$

5. ESTIMATION

If we wish to estimate the result of a calculation it is often helpful to work to an accuracy of one significant figure (s.f.), using standard form where appropriate. We use the symbol $\approx$ for 'is approximately equal to'.

Example 5

(a) A rough estimate of the cost of 312 text books costing £1.95 each is $300 \times £2 = £600$.

(b) The time for light to travel (at 299 000 km/s) from a star to one of its planets (a distance of 212 000 000 km) is

$$\frac{212\,000\,000}{299\,000} \text{ s.}$$

This might be estimated as

$$\frac{2 \times 10^8}{3 \times 10^5} \text{s} = \frac{2}{3} \times 10^3 \text{ s} \approx 0.7 \times 10^3 \text{ s} = 7 \times 10^{-1} \times 10^3 \text{ s}$$

$$= 7 \times 10^2 \text{ s} \quad = 700 \text{ s}$$

$$\left(or \quad \frac{2 \times 10^8}{3 \times 10^5} \text{s} = \frac{20 \times 10^7}{3 \times 10^5} \text{s} \approx 7 \times 10^2 \text{ s} = 700 \text{ s} \right).$$

Here are some further examples of estimates of answers to calculations.

Example 6

(a) $0.00835 \times 197\,000 \approx 8 \times 10^{-3} \times 2 \times 10^5 = 8 \times 2 \times 10^{-3} \times 10^5$
$$= 16 \times 10^{-3+5} = 16 \times 10^2 = 1600$$

(b) $\dfrac{0.000\,365}{0.0809} \approx \dfrac{4 \times 10^{-4}}{8 \times 10^{-2}} = \dfrac{4}{8} \times \dfrac{10^{-4}}{10^{-2}} = 0.5 \times 10^{-4--2}$
$$= 0.5 \times 10^{-2} = 0.005$$

or

$$\dfrac{0.000\,365}{0.0809} \approx \dfrac{40 \times 10^{-5}}{8 \times 10^{-2}} = \dfrac{40}{8} \times \dfrac{10^{-5}}{10^{-2}} = 5 \times 10^{-5--2}$$
$$= 5 \times 10^{-3} = 0.005$$

Exercise E

(No calculating aids should be used in this exercise.)

*1   Estimate to an accuracy of one significant figure:

(a) the cost of 2036 jiggits at 49 p each;

(b) the volume of a water tank with rectangular base and sides measuring
2.04 m × 3.93 m × 1.47 m;

(c) the average speed of a car which covers a distance of 244 km in 4 hours 3 minutes;

(d) the number of fluffed wheat flakes in a packet containing 250 g of fluffed wheat
if the average mass of a flake is 3.27 mg.

2   Estimate, to an accuracy of one significant figure, the values of:

(a) 205×0.98 (b) $334 \times 68\,000$ (c) 535×475

(d) $0.006\,94 \times 0.423$ (e) $1.007\,65 \times 1.013\,02$

(f) $2.37 \times 10^{19} \times 2.96 \times 10^{-12}$

*3   Estimate, to an accuracy of one significant figure, the values of:

(a) $\dfrac{205}{0.98}$ (b) $\dfrac{334}{68\,000}$ (c) $\dfrac{68\,000}{334}$ (d) $\dfrac{535}{475}$ (e) $\dfrac{0.006\,94}{0.423}$

(f) $\dfrac{1.007\,65}{1.013\,02}$ (g) $\dfrac{2.37 \times 10^{19}}{2.96 \times 10^{-12}}$ (h) $\dfrac{0.279}{0.0812}$

4   Estimate, to an accuracy of one significant figure, the values of:

(a) $325\,000 \times 0.007\,98$ (b) $\dfrac{0.0468}{0.000\,983}$ (c) $200\,100 \div 0.0375$

(d) $897.6 \times \dfrac{273}{283} \times \dfrac{0.765}{0.747}$ (e) $\dfrac{110\,100 \times 0.000\,007\,72}{0.0416}$ (f) $\dfrac{1}{19.93}$

*5   The mass of the earth is about 6×10^{24} kg and the mass of an electron is
about 9×10^{-31} kg. Roughly how many electrons are equivalent in mass to the mass
of the earth?

6   The radius of the earth is about 6×10^6 m. The surface area of a sphere of radius R
is about $12.6\,R^2$. Roughly what is the surface area of the earth?

*7   If the charge on an electron is 1.6×10^{-19} coulomb, what is the approximate number
of electrons passing a given point in a wire in a millionth of one second, if the wire is
carrying a current of 3×10^{-6} amp (i.e. 3×10^{-6} coulomb/s)?

8   One light-year is the distance that light travels in one year. Roughly how many kilometres away is a star which is at a distance of 47 light-years? (The speed of light is
3×10^8 m/s.)

9 10^{-6} s is known as a microsecond (μs) and 10^{-9} s as a nanosecond (ns). Roughly how many nanoseconds does light take to travel the length of your classroom? After how many microseconds, approximately, will you see a flash of lightning 10 km away?

6. IS YOUR ANSWER SENSIBLE?

When you have a problem to solve it is important to consider whether your answer is realistic. If it is not, you should check your method or working.

Sometimes it may be straightforward to decide whether an answer is reasonable. For example, answers of 5 km for the height of a house or 6 cm^2 for the area of a football pitch are clearly incorrect. In other cases it may be more difficult, but we may be able to obtain a rough estimate for the answer by 'scaling-up' or 'scaling-down'.

Example 7
Estimate the thickness of a sheet of typing-paper.

A box containing 500 sheets of such paper is about 4 cm deep, so the paper is about $\dfrac{4}{500}$ cm $= \dfrac{8}{1000}$ cm $= 0.008$ cm $= 0.08$ mm.

Example 8
Estimate how many bricks can be carried by a lorry of capacity 5 m^3.

A brick has dimensions of about 23 cm by 12 cm by 8 cm. Its volume is therefore approximately $23 \times 12 \times 8$ cm$^3 \approx 2200$ cm^3. The lorry could carry

$$\frac{5 \times 10^6}{2200} = \frac{5}{2.2} \times 10^3 \approx 2.3 \times 10^3 = 2300 \text{ bricks.}$$

Exercise F

1 Estimate the following measurements:
  (*a*) the width of your thumb-nail;
  (*b*) the diameter of a 10p coin;
  (*c*) your height;
  (*d*) the length of the sole of one of your shoes.

2 Estimate the following:
  (*a*) your mass;
  (*b*) the mass of this book;
  (*c*) the mass of a car;
  (*d*) the mass of a pencil.

3 Estimate the areas of the following:
  (*a*) a page of this book;
  (*b*) a football pitch;
  (*c*) your classroom;
  (*d*) a postage stamp.

4 Estimate the volumes of the following:
  (*a*) the air in your classroom;
  (*b*) a cup of tea;
  (*c*) this book;
  (*d*) a sugar lump.

5 Estimate the following:
  (*a*) the volume of a match-box;
  (*b*) the volume of a matchstick;
  (*c*) the thickness of a matchstick;
  (*d*) the number of match-boxes which would fill your classroom.

6 Estimate the following:
  (*a*) the volume of a pack of playing-cards;
  (*b*) the thickness of a playing-card;
  (*c*) the area of one side of a playing-card;
  (*d*) the volume of a storage-space required in a warehouse to store 10 000 packs of cards.

7 (*a*) Roughly what area is required for a car-park for 100 cars?
  (*b*) Roughly what is the height of a three-storey building?
  (*c*) Roughly what is the total printed area of a newspaper?
  (*d*) Roughly what is the total area of paintwork in the classrooms in your school?

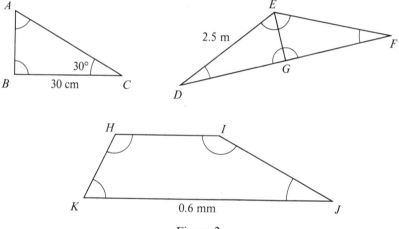

Figure 2

8 Assuming that each of the diagrams in Figure 2 is drawn approximately to scale, estimate roughly the lengths of all unlabelled sides and the sizes of all unlabelled angles. Estimate also the areas of
  (*a*) triangle *ABC*;   (*b*) triangle *DEF*;   (*c*) quadrilateral *HIJK*.

9 Figure 3 shows the approximate position of a mysterious comet in relation to the sun and α Centauri, which are 4.3 light-years apart. Estimate roughly the distance between the comet and the sun.

10 Figure 4 shows the connecting points (as dots) on a silicon chip, the dimensions of which are given. Estimate the approximate distance between connecting points *P* and *Q*.

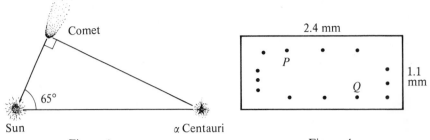

Figure 3   Figure 4

SUMMARY

$10^a \times 10^b = 10^{(a+b)}$ and $10^a \div 10^b = 10^{(a-b)}$

$10^0 = 1$

$10^{-a} = \dfrac{1}{10^a}$ (Section 1)

A number in 'standard form' is written as $A \times 10^n$ where n is an integer and $1 \leqslant A < 10$. For example,

(a) $21\,000 = 2.1 \times 10^4$
(b) $0.0052 \stackrel{\bullet}{=} 5.2 \times 10^{-3}$

(Section 2)

Units

Mass   1 kg = 1000 g = 10^6 mg
       1 g = 10^{-3} kg;   1 mg = 10^{-6} kg
       1 tonne = 1000 kg

Length   1 m = 100 cm = 1000 mm
         1 cm = 10^{-2} m;   1 mm = 10^{-3} m
         1 km = 1000 m

Area   1 ha = 10^4 m^2
       1 km^2 = 100 ha

Volume   1 l = 1 dm^3 = 1000 cm^3
(fluid)   1 l = 100 cl = 1000 ml
          1 ml = 10^{-3} l   (Section 3)

Rough estimates of the results of calculations, to an accuracy of one significant figure, can be made using standard form as a help. For example,

$$\frac{0.006\,21}{0.0287} \approx \frac{6 \times 10^{-3}}{3 \times 10^{-2}} = \frac{6}{3} \times \frac{10^{-3}}{10^{-2}} = 2 \times 10^{-3--2}$$
$$= 2 \times 10^{-1} = 0.2$$

(Sections 4, 5)

You should make sure that your answers to practical problems are reasonable.   (Section 6)

Summary exercise

1 Simplify, using indices:
   (a) $10^4 \times 10^7$ (b) $10^7 \div 10^4$ (c) $10^4 \div 10^7$
   (d) $10^4 \times 10^{-7}$ (e) $10^{-2} \times 10^{-4}$ (f) $10^{-3} \div 10^{-5}$
   (g) $\dfrac{10^2 \times 10^{-3}}{10^4 \times 10^{-5}}$ (h) $\dfrac{1}{10^{-2}}$

2 Simplify:
   (a) $10^2 + 10^3$ (b) $10^{-1} + 10^{-2}$

3 Write each of the following numbers in standard form:
   (a) 200·000   (b) 0.0007   (c) 390.5   (d) 0.000 0682

4 Write each of these numbers in full, not in standard form:
   (a) 2.36×10^{-5} (b) 8.20×10^4
   (c) $0.006\,45 \times 10^6$ (d) 28.3×10^{-3}

5 Express the following distances in standard form in metres:
   (a) 38.6 mm;   (b) 0.15 cm;   (c) 17.5 km;   (d) 1.86×10^6 km.

6 Express the following masses in standard form in kilograms:
   (a) 381 g;   (b) 36 tonne;   (c) 2.0 mg;   (d) 0.86 g;   (e) 39 400 kg.

7 (a) Express the following volumes in standard form in cubic metres:
      (i) 3.85 cm^3;   (ii) 0.5 cm^3.
   (b) Express the following volumes of fluids in standard form in litres:
      (i) 420 ml;   (ii) 500 cm^3.

8 Estimate, to an accuracy of one significant figure, the value of:
   (a) $215\,000 \times 0.000\,774$ (b) $\dfrac{0.003\,02}{0.139}$
   (c) $486 \times \dfrac{273}{293} \times \dfrac{0.765}{0.760}$ (d) $\dfrac{1}{350}$

9 State, with reasons, whether the following statements seem reasonable or not.
   (a) The mass of water in the swimming-pool at Sampsey High School is 7.46 tonne.
   (b) The volume of coffee drunk by the 50 staff at the school each morning is about 12 l.
   (c) The area of the school playing-fields is 1 hectare.
   (d) The time taken for an aircraft to fly from the North Pole to the South Pole was 9 hours 47 minutes, excluding refuelling stops.

Miscellaneous exercise

1 The amount of water in all the oceans of the world has been estimated as about 10^{23} l. The number of molecules in a litre of water is estimated to be about 10^{26}. How many molecules of water are there in all the oceans of the world?

2 The Great Pyramid of Gizeh contains over two million stone blocks averaging about 2500 kg each in mass. Estimate the total mass of stone used to build the pyramid.

3 How long does it take light to travel from the sun to the planet Saturn? (Speed of light $\approx 300\,000$ km/s; mean distance from Saturn to the sun $\approx 1.4 \times 10^9$ km.)

4 Subtract 8.3×10^{-4} kg from 4.215×10^{-2} kg and give the answer:
   (a) in kilograms, in standard form;   (b) in grams.

5 Arrange each of the following sets of measurements in order of magnitude, writing the largest first:

   (a) 37×10^{-4} cm,   0.42 mm, 2.8×10^{-4} m,   0.000 73 m,   0.05 cm;

   (b) 50 000 g,   7.8 kg, 10^6 mg,   0.1 tonne, 10^4 g.

6 The mass of 6.0×10^{23} atoms of copper is 0.089 kg. Estimate the mass of an atom of copper.

7 If you live to be 100 years old, for how many seconds will you have lived? Estimate the mass of food you will have eaten in that time.

8 The force of attraction, measured in newtons, between the moon and the earth, is given by the formula $\dfrac{GmM}{r^2}$, where

   G, the gravitational constant $\approx 6.7 \times 10^{-11}$ N m/kg,

   M, the mass of the earth $\approx 6.0 \times 10^{24}$ kg,

   m, the mass of the moon $\approx 7.3 \times 10^{22}$ kg,

   r, the mean distance between the earth and the moon $\approx 3.8 \times 10^{10}$ m.

   Estimate this force of attraction. How does it compare with the force attracting you towards the centre of the earth which, in newtons, is about ten times your mass in kilograms?

9 Small distances may be measured in micrometres (μm). $1\ \mu\text{m} = 10^{-6}$ m. If interconnecting lines on a silicon chip for a computer can be manufactured with a distance of only 0.4 μm between them, how many parallel lines can be placed across a chip of width 5 mm?

10 Estimate the thickness of this page in micrometres. ($1\ \mu\text{m} = 10^{-6}$ m.)

3

Using a calculator

1. DOES IT AGREE WITH YOU?

Calculate $2 + 3 \times 4$. Now use your calculator to do the same calculation. Do you both agree that the answer is 14?

When calculating arithmetical expressions, the following conventions apply:

(1) contents of brackets are calculated first;

(2) powers are calculated before multiplication and division; addition and subtraction are performed last;

(3) in the absence of any of these priorities, expressions are calculated from left to right.

So, for example,

$$10 - 3^2 = 10 - 9 = 1$$
$$(10 - 3)^2 = 7^2 = 49$$
$$8 + 6 \div 2 = 8 + 3 = 11$$
$$(8 + 6) \div 2 = 14 \div 2 = 7$$

Can you make your calculator agree with these?

Exercise A

(*a*) Calculate the following without using your calculator.

(*b*) Check your answers with the answers at the back of the book.

(*c*) Obtain the answers using your calculator, doing no part of the calculation in your head. If your calculator has a memory or a key for squaring, make sure that you discover how best to use them in working out the problems. (If your calculator does not have a memory you may need to write down an answer to part of a calculation before you can continue.)

*1	$2 + 4 - 3$	***2**	$2 \times 3 + 4$	***3**	$2 \times (3 + 4)$
*4	$\dfrac{3 \times 4}{2}$	***5**	$\dfrac{3 + 4}{2}$	***6**	$12 - 4 + 2$
*7	$12 - 4 - 2$	***8**	$12 - 4 \times 2$	***9**	$12 - (4 - 2)$
*10	$\dfrac{12}{4 + 2}$	***11**	$\dfrac{12}{4 - 2}$	***12**	$\dfrac{12}{4 \times 2}$
*13	$3^2 + 4.$	***14**	$3 + 4^2$	***15**	$3^2 + 4^2$
*16	$(3 + 4)^2$	***17**	$17 - 3^2$	***18**	$4^2 - 3^2$
*19	$(5 - 3)^2$	***20**	3×2^2	***21**	$(3 \times 2)^2$
*22	$3^2 \times 2^2$	***23**	$12 \div 2^2$	***24**	$3 \times 6 + 2 \times 5$

How accurate is your calculator?

When 2 is divided by 3, the answer in decimals should be 0.666 666 666 666 ... , with the sixes going on for ever. We write this as 0.6̇ and call it 'zero point six recurring'.

When you divide 2 by 3 on your calculator, how many decimal places are shown on the display? Calculators usually work to more decimal places than are displayed, but they cannot store the whole of a recurring decimal. They are designed to do one of two things: either they will 'truncate', i.e. cut the end off the number, or they will 'round off', i.e. give the number corrected to the number of figures in the display. A calculator which displays six decimal places and 'truncates' would give 0.6̇ as 0.666 666 and 0.9̇ as 0.999 999 while a calculator which 'rounds off' would give 0.6̇ as 0.666 667 and 0.9̇ as 1. Both sorts would give 0.3̇ as 0.333 333; can you see why?

Exercise B

(a) Calculate the following as decimals without using your calculator.

(b) Check your answers with the answers at the back of the book.

(c) Obtain the answers using your calculator. If your calculator has a reciprocal key, discover how best to use it.

*1 $\frac{1}{2}$ ***2** $\frac{1}{3+7}$ ***3** $\frac{1}{6}$ ***4** $(1 \div 6) \times 6$ ***5** $\frac{5}{6}$

*6 $(1 \div 6) \times 5$ ***7** $\frac{1}{6} + \frac{1}{6}$ ***8** $(1 \div 3) \times 3$ ***9** $(1 \div 7) \times 7$ ***10** $(1 \div 9) \times 9$

*11 $(1 \div 9) \times 7$ ***12** $(1 \div 7) \times 21$ ***13** $\frac{2}{3} \times \frac{3}{4}$ ***14** $12 \times \frac{1}{2} \times \frac{1}{3}$ ***15** $\frac{3}{5} \div \frac{2}{10}$

You will now realise that for some calculations you can rely on all the decimal places which your calculator can give, while for others, the last one or two places of decimals may be unreliable because of errors from rounding off or truncating.

When doing a calculation, do not give the answer to more places of decimals than you can be confident are reliably accurate.

If, knowing your calculator, you decide to give your answer to fewer decimal places than the machine displays, be sure to round off and not to truncate.

Negative numbers

Can your calculator cope with negative numbers? (It does not matter too much if it cannot, but it is important to discover to what extent it can.)

Exercise C

(a) Calculate the following without using your calculator.

(b) Check your answers with the answers at the back of the book.

(c) Obtain the answers using your calculator. If your calculator has a 'change sign' $(+/-)$ key, discover how best to use it.

*1 $1-2$ ***2** $1-{}^-2$ ***3** ${}^-2+{}^-3$ ***4** ${}^-2-{}^-3$ ***5** ${}^-2\times3$

*6 $2\times{}^-3$ ***7** ${}^-2\times{}^-3$ ***8** $\dfrac{6}{{}^-2}$ ***9** $\dfrac{{}^-12}{{}^-4}$ ***10** $({}^-3)^2$

2. ESTIMATES

When you are doing problems involving less convenient numbers, it is a good idea to make a check by estimating the answer to an accuracy of one significant figure.

Example 1

Estimate the answer to the calculation below and then work it out using your calculator:

$$\frac{2.35+7.91}{9.02-5.86}$$

Estimate: $\dfrac{2.35+7.91}{9.02-5.86}\approx\dfrac{2+8}{9-6}=\dfrac{10}{3}\approx3$

(With practice this can be done in your head.)
By calculator, the result is 3.246 8354.

Example 2

Calculate the area of a floor, measuring 7.93 m by 4.82 m, left uncovered by a carpet on it of area 30.2 m².

The exposed area is $(7.93\times4.82-30.2)$ m².
Estimate: $8\times5-30=10\,\text{m}^2$
By calculator: $8.0226\,\text{m}^2=8.02\,\text{m}^2$ to 3 s.f.

Exercise D

*1   Estimate the answer to each of the following calculations and then work them out using your calculator.

(a) $2.1+3.9+3.2$

(b) $2.1+3.9-3.2$

(c) $2.2\times3.8\times2.9$

(d) $\dfrac{3.4\times3.9}{1.8}$

(e) $4.3\times5.9+1.6$

(f) $4.3\times(5.9+1.6)$

(g) $(4.3+5.9)\times1.6$

(h) $\dfrac{11.7}{2.2\times2.8}$

(i) $6.8+1.3\times4.5$

(j) $12.9-2.1\times3.8$

(k) $12.9-(4.6-3.7)$

(l) $12.9-4.6-3.7$

*2   Estimate the answer to each of the following calculations and then work them out using your calculator.

(a) $2.8\times5.9+1.9\times5.1$ (b) $2.8\times5.9-1.9\times5.1$

(c) $7.1^2+5.6$ (d) $7.1+5.6^2$

(e) $17.1-5.6^2$ (f) $7.1^2+5.6^2$

(g) $(7.1+5.6)^2$ (h) $7.1^2-5.6^2$

(i) $(7.1 - 5.6)^2$ (j) $(5.4 \times 2.9)^2$

(k) 5.4×2.9^2 (l) $(5.4)^2 \times (2.9)^2$

3   Estimate the answers to each of the following calculations and then work them out using your calculator.

(a) $\dfrac{1}{0.52}$ (b) $\dfrac{1}{(4.8 + 5.3)}$ (c) $1 + \dfrac{1}{3.95}$

(d) $2.2 + \dfrac{1}{0.59}$ (e) $\dfrac{13.9}{(2.1 + 4.9)}$ (f) $\dfrac{(3.16 + 5.22)}{(7.97 - 1.93)}$

(g) $\dfrac{1}{3.86} + \dfrac{1}{1.97}$ (h) $\dfrac{2.11}{5.07} - \dfrac{3.88}{11.6}$ (i) $\dfrac{2.11}{5.07} \times \dfrac{3.88}{11.6}$

(j) $13.9 \times \dfrac{1}{0.98} \times \dfrac{1}{1.93}$ (k) $\dfrac{6.2}{9.3} \div \dfrac{1.9}{8.8}$ (l) $\dfrac{4.91}{11.2} + \dfrac{15.3}{28.7}$

4   If $p = 1.73$, $q = 2.81$, $r = {}^-1.54$, $s = {}^-3.06$, evaluate each of the following expressions, using your calculator to help you:

(a) $p - q$;   (b) $p - s$;   (c) $r + s$;   (d) $r - s$;   (e) qs;

(f) rp;   (g) rs;   (h) $\dfrac{p}{r}$;   (i) s^2;   (j) $p(q + r)$;

(k) $pq + pr$;   (l) $(p + q)(r + s)$;   (m) $pq + pr + qr + rs$;   (n) $pqrs$.

*5   What is the total cost of 35 snoggins at £1.29, 146 baggits at £0.78 and 88 flumps at £2.14?

6   Average speed can be calculated as the total distance travelled divided by the total time taken. If I travel 287.5 km in 5 hours 26 minutes, calculate my average speed in kilometres per hour.

*7   If I take the *Daily Nation*, costing 12p, every day except Sunday, the *Sunday Nation*, costing 27p, and the *Keep Fit Weekly*, costing 45p per week, what should my February bill be?

8   A tin of beans, advertised as containing 447 g of beans, costs 16p. A smaller tin, containing 223 g of beans, costs 9p. How much will I save by buying 3 dozen of the larger size rather than 6 dozen of the smaller? How much extra mass of baked beans will I have?

3. SQUARES AND SQUARE ROOTS

Check that you and your calculator agree that $3^2 = 9$. Notice also that
$$(3 \times 10^5)^2 = 3 \times 10^5 \times 3 \times 10^5 = 9 \times 10^{10},$$
that $(3 \times 10^{-4})^2 = 3 \times 10^{-4} \times 3 \times 10^{-4} = 9 \times 10^{-8}$,
and that $({}^-3)^2 = 9$.

We can describe 3 as 'the positive square root of 9', written $\sqrt{9}$, because $3^2 = 9$. Since $({}^-3)^2 = 9$ also, there are two square roots of 9: $\sqrt{9} = 3$ and ${}^-\sqrt{9} = {}^-3$. Similarly there are two square roots of 49, 7 and ${}^-7$, since $7^2 = ({}^-7)^2 = 49$. We write $\sqrt{49} = 7$.

Here are some more examples:

$\sqrt{400} = 20$

$\sqrt{(9 \times 10^{10})} = 3 \times 10^5$

$\sqrt{(9 \times 10^{-8})} = 3 \times 10^{-4}$

$\sqrt{9\,000\,000} = \sqrt{(9 \times 10^6)} = 3 \times 10^3 = 3000$

$$\sqrt{0.000\,004} = \sqrt{(4 \times 10^{-6})} = 2 \times 10^{-3} = 0.002$$
$$\sqrt{250\,000} = \sqrt{(2.5 \times 10^5)} = \sqrt{(25 \times 10^4)} = 5 \times 10^2 = 500$$
$$\sqrt{0.000\,016} = \sqrt{(1.6 \times 10^{-5})} = \sqrt{(16 \times 10^{-6})} = 4 \times 10^{-3} = 0.004$$

Look at the last two examples particularly carefully. Notice that when using standard form, if we want to find the square root, this involves halving the power of ten. This means that sometimes the number may have to be re-written so that the power is even.

Exercise E

*1 Write down the positive square roots of the following numbers:
    (a) 64   (b) 121   (c) 169   (d) 196
    (e) 40 000 (f) 900   (g) 0.04 (h) 0.0009

*2 Write down the positive square roots of the following numbers:
    (a) 640 000   (b) 36 000 000   (c) 8.1×10^{11} (d) 4.9×10^{17}
    (e) 0.0064   (f) 0.000 000 36   (g) 2.5×10^{-7} (h) 1.6×10^{-19}

*3 Use $\sqrt{3} \approx 1.73$ and $\sqrt{30} \approx 5.48$ to write down the approximate square roots of:
    (a) 300   (b) 3000   (c) 3×10^8 (d) 3×10^7
    (e) 0.3   (f) 0.0003   (g) 3×10^{-7} (h) 3×10^{-11}

4 Use $\sqrt{5} \approx 2.24$ and $\sqrt{50} \approx 7.07$ to write down the approximate square roots of:
    (a) 5000   (b) 5 million   (c) 5×10^{13} (d) 5×10^{12}
    (e) 0.5   (f) 0.0005   (g) 5×10^{-13} (h) 5×10^{-12}

4. DECIMAL SEARCH

Many calculators have a special key (usually marked $\sqrt{x}$) for finding square roots. If we wanted to find $\sqrt{40}$ without using such a key, we could proceed as follows:

$6^2 = 36$ and $7^2 = 49$ so $\sqrt{40}$ is between 6 and 7;
$6.1^2 = 37.21$
$6.2^2 = 38.44$
$6.3^2 = 39.69$
$6.4^2 = 40.96$ so $\sqrt{40}$ is between 6.3 and 6.4;
$6.31^2 = 39.8161$
$6.32^2 = 39.9424$
$6.33^2 = 40.0689$ so $\sqrt{40}$ is between 6.32 and 6.33

and so on.

By this method, known as 'decimal search', we can approach nearer and nearer to the value of $\sqrt{40}$, stopping when we no longer require greater accuracy.

Since $2^3 = 2 \times 2 \times 2 = 8$, the *cube root* of 8 is 2. We write $\sqrt[3]{8} = 2$. Notice that there is only one cube root: $^-2$ is not a cube root of 8, since $(^-2)^3 = {}^-8$. Cube roots can be found by decimal search; for example, to find $\sqrt[3]{40}$ we proceed as follows:

$2^3 = 8$, $3^3 = 27$, $4^3 = 64$ so $\sqrt[3]{40}$ is between 3 and 4;

40 is nearly halfway between 27 and 64, so we could start searching for $\sqrt[3]{40}$ at 3.5;

$3.5^3 = 42.875$

$3.4^3 = 39.304$ so $\sqrt[3]{40}$ is between 3.4 and 3.5;

$3.41^3 = 39.651\ 821$

$3.42^3 = 40.001\ 688$ so $\sqrt[3]{40}$ is between 3.41 and 3.42

and so on.

(It is clear that $\sqrt[3]{40}$ is very close to 3.42, so it would probably be quickest to try 3.419 next and then 3.418 if necessary.)

Exercise F

*1   Use decimal search methods to find, to an accuracy of three significant figures:

     (a) $\sqrt{7}$ (b) $\sqrt{70}$ (c) $\sqrt[3]{20}$ (d) $\sqrt[3]{100}$

2   (a) Copy and complete the following table of cubes:

x	4	5	6	7	8	9	10
x^3					729		

    (b) Write down an estimate of $\sqrt[3]{200}$ to 1 s.f., and find its value to 2 s.f. using decimal search.

    (c) Repeat (b) for $\sqrt[3]{500}$.

3   (a) Copy and complete the following table of cubes:

x	0.1	0.2	0.3	0.4	0.5	0.6	0.7	0.8	0.9
x^3				0.064					

    (b) Write down an estimate of $\sqrt[3]{0.2}$ to 1 s.f., and find its value to 2 s.f. using decimal search.

    (c) Repeat (b) for $\sqrt[3]{0.7}$.

4   Use decimal search methods to find, to 3 s.f.:

    (a) $\sqrt[3]{0.01}$ (b) $\sqrt[3]{0.3}$

5. ESTIMATING AND CHECKING

Even with a calculator, results may be wrong. You may have made a few mistakes already! The usual reasons for wrong results are:

  (1) failing to enter a number correctly;

  (2) pressing a key twice or pressing a wrong key;

  (3) failing to clear display or stores;

  (4) missing out part of the calculation;

  (5) failing to take proper notice of brackets or failing to realise where they would go, when they are unwritten;

  (6) failing to make proper use of the '=' key;

  (7) failing fully to understand the effect of a key when you press it, especially in connection with use of memory keys;

  (8) difficulties concerned with machine overflow;

(9) almost-flat batteries;

(10) a faulty machine.

With a calculation which is long or complicated, it is best to check the result by using one or more of the following approaches:

   (a) make an estimate of the answer, working to an accuracy of one significant figure, preferably before you use the calculator;
   (b) repeat the calculation, if possible doing it in a different order;
   (c) use the answer obtained to 'calculate back' to one of the original numbers entered.

These ideas are best illustrated by an example.

Example 3

Evaluate $\dfrac{26\ 700}{386 \times 1920}$.

(a) *Make an estimate*

There are several ways of doing this. For example:

(i) $\dfrac{26\ 700}{386 \times 1920} \approx \dfrac{30\ 000}{400 \times 2000} = \dfrac{3}{80} \approx \dfrac{3}{100} = 0.03$;

(ii) $\dfrac{26\ 700}{386 \times 1920} \approx \dfrac{3 \times 10^4}{4 \times 10^2 \times 2 \times 10^3} = \dfrac{30}{8} \times 10^{-2} \approx 4 \times 10^{-2}$

$$= 0.04.$$

(b) *The calculation*

You should first choose the method you feel to be the most straightforward. A suitable order of operations, here, is shown in Figure 1. The result is 0.036 03, to 4 s.f.

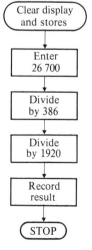

Figure 1

Repeating the calculation in a different way

In checking by an alternative method, you should expect that you may not obtain perfect agreement in the last one or even two figures of an 8-figure display. If agreement is not good, however, careful thought must be given as to which method of calculation is the more accurate. Another approach to this calculation, using a memory (or a piece of paper) is shown in the flow chart in Figure 2.

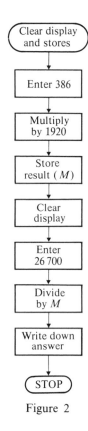

Figure 2

(c) *Using the answer*

If the process for doing the calculation can be represented by a simple flow chart and does not involve the use of a memory, you can easily 'calculate back' from the answer displayed to the first number entered, using inverse operations and reversing the flow chart. This tends to be a fairly time-consuming method of checking, since the flow chart must be outlined first, but it is useful when several calculations of the same type have to be performed. Of course, if the original flow chart is wrong, the reversed flow chart will not reveal this error.

For the calculation $\dfrac{26\ 700}{386 \times 1920} \approx 0.036\ 03$ we have the flow charts in Figure 3.

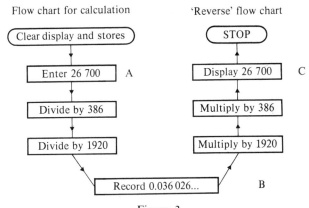

Figure 3

(The last two figures of the answer obtained at point B may vary from one calculator to another and the agreement between A and C may not be particularly close. For example, one calculator gave 26 699.959 at C.)

Exercise G

(*a*) Without the calculator, make an estimate of the answers to the calculations below, working to an accuracy of one significant figure.

(*b*) Use your calculator to work out the calculations. Where possible, work out each calculation by two different methods as a check.

(*c*) For some of the questions, check the answers by calculating back to the first number entered, using a 'reverse' flow chart.

* 1	$3.05 \times 0.0792 \times 610$	2	$\dfrac{12.9 \times 0.064}{203}$
* 3	$3.57(86.3 - 21.9)$	4	$\dfrac{7.06}{2.19 \times 3.58}$
* 5	$0.061 - 0.0085 \times 2.14$	6	$2.3 \times 0.087 - 1.5 \times 0.066$
* 7	$2.82^2 - 1.19^2$	8	$(2.82 - 1.19)^2$
* 9	438×0.86^2	10	$\dfrac{1}{0.0815}$
*11	$\dfrac{8.25 \times 0.064}{2.13 - 0.79}$	12	$\dfrac{1}{0.007\,82} + \dfrac{1}{0.0103}$
*13	$\sqrt{0.000\,789}$	14	$\sqrt{(3.52 - 2.71)}$
*15	$\sqrt{0.81} - \sqrt{0.72}$	16	$\sqrt{(4.78^2 + 2.19^2)}$
*17	0.369^3	18	$\left(\dfrac{0.064}{3.20}\right)^2$
*19	$0.604 - \sqrt{2.19}$	20	$32.8 - (17.9 - 24.6)$
*21	$0.36(8.5 - 10.3)$	22	$\dfrac{0.082 - 0.106}{11.7 - 15.8}$
*23	$\dfrac{1}{(20.10 - 31.60)^2}$	24	$8.64 \times \dfrac{273}{293} \times \dfrac{0.0185}{0.0210}$

SUMMARY

To remind yourself how best to use your calculator, experiment with easy numbers which allow you to forecast confidently the result of the type of calculation concerned.   (Section 1)

Three methods of checking calculations performed on the calculator are recommended:
   (i) make an estimate, working to an accuracy of one significant figure;
   (ii) repeat the calculation, preferably in a different order;
   (iii) 'calculate back' from the answer to one of the original values.

(Sections 2, 5)

If $a^2 = b$ then a and ^-a are the square roots of b. The positive square root of b is written $\sqrt{b}$.

If $c^3 = b$ then $c = \sqrt[3]{b}$, the cube root of b.

Roots can be found by decimal search.   (Sections 3, 4)

Summary exercise

1   Estimate the following and then use your calculator to obtain an answer accurate to five significant figures:

(a) $13.72 + 5.91 \times 12.34$ (b) $\dfrac{497}{53.2 - 34.5}$

(c) $49.2^2 - 41.3^2$ (d) $\dfrac{1}{0.037} + 5.71$

(e) $\dfrac{12.57 + 37.61}{4.17 - 12.12}$

2   Make an estimate of the answers to the calculations below, using standard form to help you. Use your calculator to work out the answers, giving all figures displayed in the answer. Check your results in some appropriate way, trying to obtain greater accuracy.

(a) $138 \times 0.006\,25 - 129 \times 0.004\,37$ (b) $\dfrac{1}{0.000\,964} - \dfrac{1}{0.000\,375}$

(c) $\dfrac{0.000\,219 \times 0.000\,186}{82.73 - 64.19}$ (d) $\dfrac{0.000\,197}{3971} \times 688$

(e) $\dfrac{0.000\,219 + 0.000\,186}{82.73 + 64.19}$

3   Use a decimal search method to find, to 3 s.f.:
   (a) $\sqrt[3]{24}$;   (b) $\sqrt[3]{0.4}$.

Miscellaneous exercise

1   In 1980, 47 members of St Astrid's school contributed £1.75 each towards the cost of a record player. How much should each of a further 34 members of the school be asked to contribute in 1981 if the record player costs £129.95?

2   It is estimated that the times taken for 100 people to leave through each of five exit doors to a concert hall are, in an emergency, 84 s, 77 s, 75 s, 62 s, 41 s, respectively.

Calculate how many people can leave per second through each door, on average, to 3 s.f. If people always go to the door where there is the least queue (so that no doorway is vacant while there are still people in the hall) what is the least time necessary for 3520 people to leave the hall?

3 A staircase with 19 stairs has treads with dimensions as shown. Calculate what length of stair carpet is required. What will the cost be if the carpet (of the appropriate width) which I choose, costs £4.99 per metre?

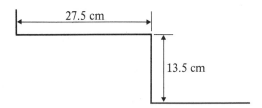

27.5 cm

13.5 cm

4 (a) Check that you agree that $\dfrac{12}{2 \times 3}$ is the same as:

$$12 \div (2 \times 3) = (12 \div 2) \div 3 = (12 \div 3) \div 2 = \frac{1}{(2 \times 3) \div 12} = \frac{1}{2 \times 3} \times 12$$

Use each of these versions as the basis of a different method of evaluating $\dfrac{12}{2 \times 3}$ using your calculator, writing down the key sequences you use. Do you always obtain exactly the same answer? (*Note*. If your calculator has a reciprocal key $\left(\dfrac{1}{x}\right)$, this should be used for the last two versions of the calculation.)

(b) Complete each of the following calculations in all the different ways suggested by the various equivalent versions given.

(i) $\dfrac{2.5}{3.2} \times \dfrac{9.8}{1.7} = (2.5 \div 3.2) \times (9.8 \div 1.7)$

$= (2.5 \times 9.8) \div (3.2 \times 1.7)$

$= 2.5 \div 3.2 \times 9.8 \div 1.7$

$= \dfrac{1}{3.2 \times 1.7} \times 2.5 \times 9.8$

(ii) $\dfrac{7.9}{8.3 + 1.6} = 7.9 \div (8.3 + 1.6) = \dfrac{1}{8.3 + 1.6} \times 7.9$

$= \dfrac{1}{(8.3 + 1.6) \div 7.9}$

(c) Write each of the calculations below in as many different forms as possible, as in the previous examples, and then complete the calculations in each of the different ways these suggest.

(i) $5.78 \times \dfrac{2.19}{6.18}$ (ii) $\dfrac{9.73 - 5.18}{6.02 \times 0.97}$

5 Do you know your calculator now? Read through the key sequences given below and forecast what your calculator will display after each key is pressed. If your calculator gives an unexpected display try to find out why.

  Experiment with other simple key sequences like these, trying to forecast the display after each key is pressed.

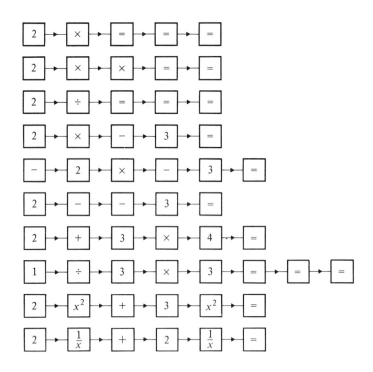

4

The language of algebra

1. ALGEBRAIC EXPRESSIONS

Algebraic expressions are often a shorthand way of writing down a rule for doing calculations. For example, a car travelling at an average speed of 50 km/h takes 2 hours to cover 100 km.

To travel 150 km it takes $\dfrac{150}{50}$ hours = 3 hours.

To travel 300 km it takes $\dfrac{300}{50}$ hours = 6 hours.

In each case, the number of kilometres travelled is divided by 50 to give the number of hours. This can be summarised by writing:

Number of hours taken to travel d km at an average speed of 50 km/h $= \dfrac{d}{50}$.

At an average speed of 60 km/h a journey of 150 km would take $\dfrac{150}{60}$ hours $= 2\frac{1}{2}$ hours; at an average speed of 30 km/h it would take $\dfrac{150}{30}$ hours = 5 hours.

The distance travelled is divided by the average speed:

Number of hours taken to travel d km at an average speed of q km/h $= \dfrac{d}{q}$.

Exercise A

*1　If one cup of coffee costs 15 pence, what is the cost in pence of:
　　(*a*) 3 cups ;　(*b*) 4 cups ;　(*c*) *n* cups?

 2　If one orange costs 4 pence, what is the cost in pence of:
　　(*a*) 5 oranges ;　(*b*) 7 oranges ;　(*c*) *q* oranges?

*3　If a pencil costs *x* pence, what is the cost in pence of:
　　(*a*) 5 pencils ;　(*b*) 15 pencils ;　(*c*) *q* pencils?

 4　If a ruler costs *R* pence, what is the cost in pence of:
　　(*a*) 3 rulers ;　(*b*) *p* rulers ;　(*c*) *r* rulers?

*5　What is the perimeter of:
　　(*a*) a triangle with sides 8 cm, 20 cm, and 15 cm ;
　　(*b*) a triangle with sides *x* cm, 12 cm, and 8 cm ;
　　(*c*) a triangle with sides *x* cm, 2*x* cm, and *y* cm?

 6　What is the perimeter of a rectangle:
　　(*a*) 12 cm long and 8 cm wide ;

(b) q cm long and 4 cm wide;

(c) l cm long and w cm wide?

*7 What is the area of each rectangle in question 6?

8 What is the volume of a cuboid:

(a) 12 cm long, 4 cm wide and 5 cm high;

(b) 12 cm long, 4 cm wide and h cm high;

(c) l cm long, w cm wide and h cm high?

*9 If petrol costs 3 francs per litre, how many litres can you buy for:

(a) 30 francs;   (b) 150 francs;   (c) n francs?

10 If petrol costs q pence per litre, how many litres can you buy for:

(a) 100 pence;   (b) 880 pence;   (c) x pence?

2. CONVENTIONS

Answering the questions of Exercise A should have reminded you of some of the conventions of algebraic language. For example:

(1) we distinguish between lower case and capital letters such as r and R;

(2) we write $15n$ rather than $n15$;

(3) we write xy rather than $x \times y$;

(4) we often, but not always, use alphabetical order.

These are really ways of making it easier for people to read each other's mathematics, and their own.

We met some other details of algebraic language in Chapter 1:

(5) we usually write $3(x - 7)$ rather than $(x - 7)3$;

(6) $\frac{1}{2}x$ can also be written as $\dfrac{x}{2}$, or printed as $x \div 2$ or $x/2$;

(7) brackets are used to specify the order in which operations are to be carried out; if there are no brackets squaring is carried out before multiplication and division, and addition and subtraction are done last. These are the same conventions as those for arithmetical expressions which were given in Chapter 3.

Example 1

Find the values of (a) $5x^2$; (b) $7(x - 2)$ when (i) $x = 6$; (ii) $x = {}^-3$.

(a) (i) When $x = 6$, $5x^2 = 5 \times 6^2 = 5 \times 36 = 180$.

(ii) When $x = {}^-3$, $5x^2 = 5 \times {}^-3^2 = 5 \times 9 = 45$.

(b) (i) When $x = 6$, $7(x - 2) = 7(6 - 2) = 7 \times 4 = 28$.

(ii) When $x = {}^-3$, $7(x - 2) = 7({}^-3 - 2) = 7 \times {}^-5 = {}^-35$.

Exercise B

*1 Find the value of $3x^2 - 7$ when:

(a) $x = 2$;   (b) $x = 0$;   (c) $x = {}^-3$;   (d) $x = {}^-\frac{1}{2}$.

2 Find the value of $\frac{1}{2}(x^2 + 1)$ when:

(a) $x = 3$;   (b) $x = {}^-5$;   (c) $x = {}^-2$;   (d) $x = {}^-\frac{1}{3}$.

*3 Find the value of $p^2 + q^2$ if:
    (a) $p = 2$ and $q = 3$;   (b) $p = {}^-1$ and $q = 4$;
    (c) $p = {}^-3$ and $q = {}^-4$;   (d) $p = \frac{1}{2}$ and $q = \frac{1}{3}$.

4 Find the value of $(p + q)^2$ if;
    (a) $p = 2$ and $q = 3$;   (b) $p = {}^-1$ and $q = 4$;
    (c) $p = {}^-3$ and $q = {}^-4$;   (d) $p = \frac{1}{2}$ and $q = \frac{1}{3}$.

*5 The area of the trapezium in Figure 1 is given by the expression
$\frac{1}{2}h(a + b)$ cm². Find the area if:
    (a) $h = 3$, $a = 4$ and $b = 10$;
    (b) $h = 5$, $a = 2$ and $b = 10$;
    (c) $h = 6$, $a = 3$ and $b = 7$;
    (d) $h = 3 \times 10^2$, $a = 2.4 \times 10^3$ and $b = 3.6 \times 10^3$.

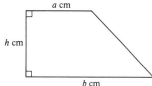

Figure 1

6 The depth of a well is approximately $5t^2$ metres, where t is the number of seconds taken by a stone to fall to the bottom of the well. Find the depth of a well if:
    (a) $t = 2$;   (b) $t = 3$;   (c) $t = 5$;   (d) $t = 5.2$.

*7 If you are standing on a cliff of height h metres, the distance you can see out to sea (on a clear day) is approximately

$$\tfrac{8}{5}\sqrt{(5h)} \text{ km}.$$

How far can you see from a cliff of height:
    (a) 20 m;   (b) 45 m;   (c) 320 m;   (d) 147 m?

8 The traffic capacity of a main road is given as $\dfrac{3600VN}{S}$ vehicles per hour, where V is the average speed of the traffic in metres per second, N is the number of traffic lanes and S is the spacing of the vehicles (front bumper to front bumper) in metres.
    (a) Find the capacity of a three-lane highway when the traffic is travelling at 20 m/s and the spacing is 80 m.
    (b) Find the capacity of a rural road with single-lane traffic travelling at 10 m/s and a spacing of 20 m.

*9 The increase in length of a strip of metal when it is heated through $\theta°C$ is given by the formula $l\alpha\theta$, where l is the original length of the strip. (α is called the coefficient of linear expansion of the metal; for copper, $\alpha \approx 0.000\,02$.)
    (a) A copper strip in a space-ship control panel has length 3 mm at 0°C. What will be its increase in length when it is heated through 100°C?
    (b) A copper wire is used for a communications link across a suspension bridge. On a winter morning, when its temperature is $^-3$°C, the length of the wire is 1500 m. What will its length be on a summer day when the temperature is 32°C?

10 The stopping distance for a car travelling at v km/h is approximately $\frac{1}{5}v + \frac{1}{200}v^2$ metres. Find the stopping distances for cars travelling at
    (a) 40 km/h;   (b) 50 km/h;   (c) 80 km/h;   (d) 100 km/h.

3. SIMPLIFICATION: THE DISTRIBUTIVE LAW

Ann bought six 7-pence stamps and Bill bought four 7-pence stamps. Ann spent 42 pence and Bill spent 28 pence, so together they spent 70 pence. But we could have calculated that without finding out how much they spent individually, since together they bought ten 7-pence stamps. The total cost in pence was

$$6 \times 7 + 4 \times 7 = (6 + 4) \times 7 = 10 \times 7 = 70.$$

If the cost of the stamps had been q pence each, Ann would have spent $6q$ pence and Bill would have spent $4q$. Their total expenditure would have been $10q$ pence. This illustrates that

$$6q + 4q = (6 + 4)q = 10q.$$

If Ann buys t stamps at 7 pence each, and Bill buys v stamps at the same price, then individually they spend $7t$ and $7v$ pence; together they buy $(t + v)$ stamps at a total cost of $7(t + v)$ pence.

$$7t + 7v = 7(t + v).$$

These are examples of the distributive law, which can be used in a number of ways to simplify expressions.

Example 2
   Write without brackets and simplify:
   (a) $3(x + 2) + 4(x + 3y)$;   (b) $5(2r - 3) - 3(3r - 4)$.

(a) Writing the expression without brackets, we have
   $3x + 6 + 4x + 12y = 7x + 12y + 6.$
(b) $5(2r - 3) - 3(3r - 4) = 10r - 15 - 9r + 12$
$$= 10r - 9r - 15 + 12$$
$$= r - 3$$

Example 3
   The charges made for the use of a copying machine are 4 pence for each of the first ten copies and 2 pence for each copy thereafter. What is the charge for n copies, if n is greater than 10?

Of the n copies, 10 are charged at 4 pence each, and the rest at 2 pence each. The number of copies charged at 2 pence is $n - 10$. The total charge is $2(n - 10) + 40$ pence $= 2n - 20 + 40$ pence $= 2n + 20$ pence.

Exercise C

*1   Write the following in a simpler form:
   (a) $3a + 4a$;   (b) $8b - 5b$;   (c) $4c + 3c - 5c$;   (d) $5d - 8d + 2d$.
   2   Write the following in a simpler form:
   (a) $5w - 2w + w$;   (b) $2x - 10x$;   (c) $4y - 7y + 5y$;   (d) $4z - 7z - 2z$.
*3   Write the following in a simpler form:
   (a) $5p + 4 - 3p + 2$;   (b) $2q - 5 - 3q + 7$;
   (c) $4r - 3s + 4s + 3r$;   (d) $3t - 7u - 5t - 2u$.

4 Write the following in a simpler form:
   (a) $3m - 6 - 2m - 3$;   (b) $5n + 6 - 5 - 4n$;
   (c) $3m - 7n + 4m + 8n$;   (d) $6m - 5n - 3n + 2m$.

*5 Write the following in a simpler form:
   (a) $\frac{1}{4}a + \frac{3}{4}a$;   (b) $\frac{3}{2}b + \frac{5}{2}b$;   (c) $\frac{3}{2}c + c$;   (d) $\frac{5}{2}d - \frac{3}{2}d$.

6 Write the following in a simpler form:
   (a) $\frac{1}{3}a + \frac{1}{3}a + \frac{1}{3}a$;   (b) $\frac{3}{4}b - \frac{1}{4}b$;   (c) $\frac{3}{4}c + \frac{1}{2}c - \frac{1}{4}c$;   (d) $\frac{1}{3}d + \frac{1}{4}d$.

*7 Write without brackets in as simple a form as possible:
   (a) $2(a + 3)$;   (b) $3(2b - 4)$;   (c) $3(2 - 3c) + 2(5c - 3)$;
   (d) $2(4d - 5) - 3(3d - 4)$.

8 Write without brackets in as simple a form as possible:
   (a) $2m + 3 - (2m + 1)$;   (b) $2(m + 1) - 2m$;
   (c) $m + 1 - (n + 1)$;   (d) $2m + 1 - (2n + 1)$.

*9 Write without brackets in as simple a form as possible:
   (a) $3(a - 7)$;   (b) $4(\frac{1}{2} - 3b)$;   (c) $5(c + \frac{1}{2}) - 4(\frac{1}{2}c + \frac{7}{8})$;
   (d) $6(3d - 4e) - 2(9d - 12e)$.

10 Write without brackets in as simple a form as possible:
   (a) $3(p - 2q)$;   (b) $2(2r + 3s) - 3(r - 2s)$;
   (c) $2(r - s) - 3(r + s)$;   (d) $\frac{1}{2}(3z - 7) - \frac{3}{4}(2z - 5)$.

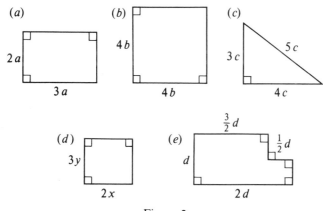

Figure 2

*11 Find in as simple a form as possible, expressions for the perimeters of the figures in Figure 2.

12 A motorist drives at an average speed of 40 km/h through built-up areas and at 90 km/h elsewhere. During a journey of 5 hours he drove through built-up areas for t hours.
   (a) For how many hours was he driving at 90 km/h?
   (b) How far did he drive through built-up areas?
   (c) How far did he drive at 90 km/h?
   (d) How far did he drive altogether? Write your answer without brackets in as simple form as possible.
   (e) Find how far he drove if (i) $t = 2$; (ii) $t = 3\frac{1}{2}$; (iii) $t = 4$.

4. SIMPLIFICATION: THE ASSOCIATIVE AND COMMUTATIVE LAWS

We can often make calculations easier by changes in the order in which we do things. For example,

$$97 + 35 + 3 = 97 + 3 + 35 = 100 + 35 = 135$$
$$25 \times 13 \times 4 = 25 \times 4 \times 13 = 100 \times 13 = 1300$$

In both these examples, we have used two important properties of addition and multiplication:

(1) the order in which two numbers are added, or multiplied, can be reversed;
$35 + 3 = 3 + 35$, $13 \times 4 = 4 \times 13$; this is the commutative law;
(2) when three numbers are added, or multiplied, it does not matter which pair is combined first; this is the associative law.

In our examples,

$$97 + (3 + 35) = (97 + 3) + 35$$
$$25 \times (4 \times 13) = (25 \times 4) \times 13$$

The commutative and associative laws can be used to simplify algebraic expressions. We have used them in Examples 2 and 3, and you will have used them in several questions in Exercise C.

Example 4
Find the area of the rectangle in Figure 3.

The area is $6a \times 4a = 6 \times a \times 4 \times a$
$= 6 \times 4 \times a \times a$
$= 24a^2$.

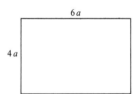

Figure 3

Example 5
Simplify:

(a) $4ab \times 5ab^2$;   (b) $\dfrac{4a^3 A^2}{6aA}$.

(a) $4ab \times 5ab^2 = 4 \times a \times b \times 5 \times a \times b \times b = 4 \times 5 \times a \times a \times b \times b \times b$
$= 20a^2 b^3$

(b) $\dfrac{4a^3 A^2}{6aA} = \dfrac{4 \times a \times a \times a \times A \times A}{6 \times a \times A} = \dfrac{2 \times a \times a \times A}{3}$

$= \tfrac{2}{3} a^2 A$ or $\dfrac{2a^2 A}{3}$

With a little practice, most of the intermediate steps can be omitted.

Exercise D

*1 Write the following in a simpler form:
(a) $2q \times 7q$;   (b) $q^2 \times q$;   (c) $3p^2 \times 4p$;   (d) $4p \times 5q$.

2 Write the following in a simpler form:
   (a) $3a \times 8a$;   (b) $ab \times a$;   (c) $2a \times 4a^3$;   (d) $5a \times 3b^2$.

*3 Write the following in a simpler form:
   (a) $p \times 2pq$;   (b) $3q \times 2pq$;   (c) $5rs \times 4rs$;   (d) $2s^2 \times 3t^2$.

4 Write the following in a simpler form:
   (a) $3p \times 5P$;   (b) $3aA \times 2A^2$;   (c) $3a^2A \times 7aA^2$;   (d) $\frac{2}{3}r \times \frac{3}{4}R^2$.

*5 Write the following in a simpler form:
   (a) $\dfrac{8m}{2}$;   (b) $\dfrac{3g}{12}$;   (c) $\dfrac{a}{a}$;   (d) $\dfrac{a^5}{a}$.

6 Write the following in a simpler form:
   (a) $\dfrac{12a}{8}$;   (b) $\dfrac{6a^2}{2a}$;   (c) $\dfrac{2a^2}{2a}$;   (d) $\dfrac{3ab}{6a}$.

*7 Write the following in a simpler form:
   (a) $\dfrac{8x^4}{2x}$;   (b) $\dfrac{42ab}{6ab}$;   (c) $\dfrac{30a^2b}{45ab}$;   (d) $\dfrac{6a^2b^2}{12ab}$.

8 Write the following in a simpler form:
   (a) $\dfrac{6a^3}{3a^2}$;   (b) $\dfrac{24ab^2}{8a}$;   (c) $\dfrac{8ab^2}{24b}$;   (d) $\dfrac{12a^2b^2}{16ab}$.

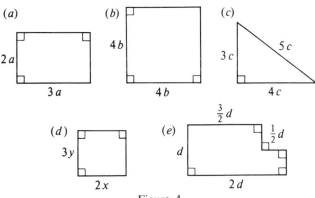

Figure 4

*9 Find, in as simple form as possible, expressions for the areas of the figures in Figure 4.

10 A farmer has 100 metres of fencing with which to construct a sheep-pen. He decides to make the pen rectangular. If the length of one side is x metres,
   (a) write down the lengths of the other three sides;
   (b) give an expression for the area of the pen;
   (c) find the area when x is
     (i) 15;   (ii) 20;   (iii) 25;   (iv) 30.
     Which value of x gives the largest area?

*11 Find, in as simple a form as possible, expressions for the volumes of the cuboids with the following dimensions:
   (a) $5x$ cm long, 3 cm wide and 4 cm high;

(b) $2q$ cm long, $3q$ cm wide and 4 cm high;

(c) $5t$ cm long, $2t$ cm wide and $6t$ cm high.

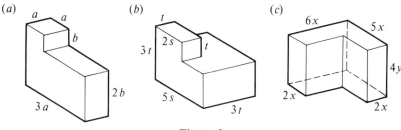

Figure 5

12   Find, in as simple a form as possible, the volumes of the solids shown in Figure 5.

5. WRITING ALGEBRAIC SENTENCES

Algebraic sentences usually involve one of the symbols:

$=$ is equal to; $\neq$ is not equal to;

$>$ is greater than; $\geq$ is greater than or equal to;

$<$ is less than; $\leq$ is less than or equal to.

A statement involving $>$, $\geq$, $<$ or $\leq$ is called an *inequality*.

Example 6

Write the following statement in symbols: The total cost of 4 cups of coffee at s pence each and 3 cups of tea at t pence each is less than 99 pence.

The total cost of the cups of coffee is $4s$ pence;

the total cost of the cups of tea is $3t$ pence.

Hence $4s + 3t < 99$.

Exercise E

In questions 1–9 write the statements as algebraic sentences:

*1   The total cost of q oranges at 7 pence each is 63 pence.

2   5 kg of potatoes at x pence per kilogram cost more than 20 pence.

*3   The perimeter of a triangle with sides of lengths a cm, b cm and 6 cm is 20 cm.

4   The area of a rectangle of length 10 cm and width w cm is less than A cm^2.

*5   The distance travelled by a car in t hours at an average speed of 60 km/h is greater than or equal to 200 km.

6   A plane flies d km in 4 hours. Its average speed is at least q km/h.

*7   The total cost of x oranges at 7 pence each and y grapefruit at 9 pence each is £ 3.40.

8   The total cost of 11 oranges at s pence each and 12 grapefruit at t pence each is more than £ 1.50.

*9   A car travelling at 60 km/h for t hours travels further than a car travelling at 50 km/h for $(t + 1)$ hours.

10 The sum of the lengths of any two sides of a triangle is greater than the length of the other side. Use this to write down three inequalities if the sides of a triangle have lengths x cm, $(x + 3)$ cm and y cm.

SUMMARY

Algebraic expressions can be used as a shorthand for a description of a calculation. (Section 1)

There are conventions, such as writing $3x$ rather than $x3$, which make mathematics easier to read. (Section 2)

The distributive, associative and commutative laws for multiplication and addition can be used to simplify expressions.

For example:

$$\left.\begin{array}{l} 3(x + 2) = 3x + 6 \\ 3x + 4x = (3 + 4)x = 7x \end{array}\right\} \text{Distributive law}$$

$$\left.\begin{array}{l} 3(4q) = (3 \times 4)q = 12q \\ p + (p + q) = (p + p) + q = 2p + q \end{array}\right\} \text{Associative law}$$

$$\left.\begin{array}{l} pq \times p = p \times pq = p^2q \\ (p + q) + p = p + (p + q) = 2p + q \end{array}\right\} \text{Commutative and associative laws}$$

(Sections 3,4)

Statements involving $>$, $\geqslant$, $<$ or $\leqslant$ are called inequalities.

(Section 5)

Summary exercise

1 Write down expression for:
   (a) the cost in pounds of x kg of apples at n pence per kilogram;
   (b) the total length in centimetres of the edges of a cuboid of length 6 cm, width y cm and height z cm.

2 Find the values of:
   (a) $2p^2 - q$ if $p = {}^-3$ and $q = {}^-4$;   (b) $3ab^2$ if $a = 2 \times 10^{-7}$ and $b = 500$.

3 Write without brackets in as simple a form as possible:
   (a) $\frac{1}{2}a - \frac{1}{3}a$;   (b) $2(7b + 10) - 5(2b - 7)$.

4 Write in as simple a form as possible:

   (a) $3a^2b^3 \times \dfrac{4a}{b^2}$;

   (b) the perimeter of Figure 6.

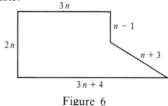

Figure 6

5 Write the following as algebraic sentences.
   (a) A car travels c km per litre of petrol. On a journey of 200 km it uses more than x litres of petrol.
   (b) Cycling 10 km at c km/h takes at least as long as walking 3 km at w km/h.

Miscellaneous exercise

1 (a) A cuboid has length 5 cm, width 4 cm and height 6 cm. Find the total area of its six faces.
   (b) Find the total area of the faces if the cuboid is $5p$ cm long, $2q$ cm wide and $3q$ cm high. Give your answer in as simple a form as possible.
   (c) What is the area in (b) if $p = 1$ and $q = 2$?

2 The cost of building a motorway in Ruritania is a million ruples per kilometre, except for the parts of the motorway which cross marshland, where the cost is two million ruples per kilometre.
   (a) The M37$\frac{1}{2}$ motorway is 43 km long, including 7 km built across marshland. How much did it cost to build?
   (b) What is the cost of building x km of motorway including y km across marshland?
   (c) Tunnelling through the Transylvanian hills costs five million ruples per kilometre. What will be the total cost of a motorway x km long, including y km across marshland and z km of tunnels?

3 An isosceles triangle has perimeter 50 cm. One of its sides is of length l cm. Write down expressions for the lengths of the other two sides. (There are two possible sets of answers.)

4 The area of an isosceles triangle with sides a cm, a cm and b cm is given by the expression $\frac{1}{4}b\sqrt{(4a^2 - b^2)}$ cm^2.
   Find this area if:
   (a) $a = 5$ and $b = 6$;
   (b) $a = 10$ and $b = 12$;
   (c) $a = 10$ and $b = 6$.

REVISION EXERCISE 2

1 Calculate:
   (a) $\frac{1}{2} + \frac{2}{3} - \frac{3}{5}$ (b) $1\frac{1}{3} \times 1\frac{1}{2}$ (c) 0.3^2 (d) $18 \div 0.3$

2 Arrange the following numbers in order of magnitude, starting with the smallest:
   $\frac{1}{3}$, $\frac{33}{100}$, 0.3, $\frac{8}{25}$.

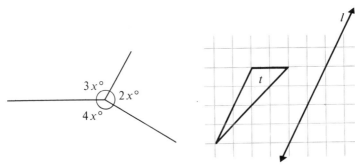

Figure 1   Figure 2

3 Calculate the value of x in Figure 1.

4 Copy Figure 2 onto squared paper and construct the image of the triangle t under reflection in the line l.

(a)   (b)   (c)

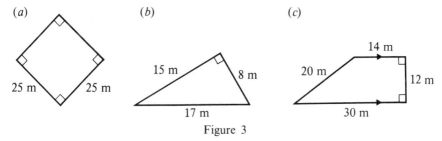

Figure 3

5 Calculate the areas of the polygons in Figure 3.

6 Draw flow charts for the functions $f: x \longrightarrow \dfrac{2x + 3}{5}$ and $g: n \longrightarrow 2\left(\dfrac{n}{5} + 3\right)$.

REVISION EXERCISE 3

1 Write in standard form:
   (a) 1984   (b) 0.000 999   (c) 20 001   (d) 0.000 07

2 Simplify, leaving your answers as powers of ten:
   (a) $10^2 \times 10^6$ (b) $10^{-3} \times 10^2$ (c) $10^4 \div 10^7$ (d) $10^{-6} \div 10^{-1}$

3 Write the following fractions as decimals:
   (a) $\frac{4}{5}$ (b) $\frac{8}{9}$ (c) $\frac{7}{8}$ (d) $\frac{5}{6}$

4 (a) How many kilograms are there in three-quarters of a tonne?
   (b) How many square metres are there in 4.7 ha ?

5 How many metres of shelving would be needed for a library of 3000 books?

6 Write down the sequence produced by the flow chart in Figure 4.

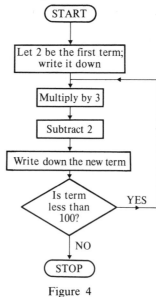

Figure 4

REVISION EXERCISE 4

1 (*a*) Calculate: (i) $1 - (0.7 + 0.07 + 0.007)$;   (ii) 25% of £25.

    (*b*) Estimate to 1 s.f.: (i) $\dfrac{30047}{0.058}$;   (ii) $\dfrac{0.000367}{0.0888}$.

2 If $p = 2 \times 10^3$ and $q = 4.9 \times 10^{-5}$, write the following numbers in standard form:

    (*a*) pq;   (*b*) $\dfrac{q}{p}$;   (*c*) $\dfrac{1}{p}$;   (*d*) $\sqrt{q}$.

3 Draw a flow chart for $f : x \longrightarrow \dfrac{25}{8 - 3x^2}$ and find $f(1)$, $f(0)$ and $f(\tfrac{1}{4})$.

4 Find the marked angles in Figure 5, in which C is the centre of the circle PQR.

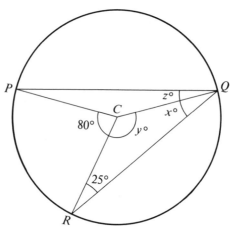

Figure 5

5 In a school of 800 pupils, three-quarters of the pupils study French and of these one-fifth also study German. One-tenth of those who do not study French study German. How many pupils study only one of these two languages?

6 Find $\sqrt[3]{2}$, correct to 3 s.f., using a decimal search method.

5

Sets

1. THE LANGUAGE OF SETS

Here is part of the list of children in form 3H in an imaginary school.

Name	Age on 1 Sept.	House	Lives more than 4 km away from school (A)	Travels to school by bus (B)	Travels to school by cycle (C)	Takes school dinner (D)
Alan Amber	13.0	Drake	Yes	No	No	Yes
Bessie Black	13.9	Drake	Yes	Yes	No	Yes
Charles Crimson	13.6	Nelson	No	Yes	No	Yes
Diana Dunn	13.2	Frobisher	Yes	No	Yes	No
Elizabeth Emerald	13.2	Benbow	No	Yes	No	Yes
Frank Fawn	13.8	Drake	Yes	No	No	Yes
Gerald Green	13.11	Benbow	Yes	No	No	Yes
Harold Heliotrope	13.0	Benbow	No	No	No	Yes
Iris Indigo	13.3	Nelson	No	No	No	Yes
James Jet	13.8	Frobisher	Yes	No	No	No
Kitty Khaki	13.5	Drake	No	No	Yes	Yes
Leslie Lilac	13.7	Nelson	No	Yes	No	Yes
Martin Mauve	13.7	Nelson	No	No	Yes	Yes
Neil Navy	13.1	Benbow	Yes	Yes	No	Yes
Olive Orange	13.10	Drake	No	No	Yes	Yes

The children on this list comprise a *set*. This is the word mathematicians use for a collection. Usually it is a collection of mathematical objects such as numbers, points, geometrical figures but the objects can be non-mathematical, such as children or file cards. The important point is that it must be possible to decide for certain whether an individual item belongs to the set or not. If it does we call it an *element* or *member* of the set.

You may have met the idea of a set before. In that case this chapter will help you to revise what you know.

Before starting to work with sets it is necessary to describe clearly the complete set we are considering. In what follows we often refer to the children in the list above. We say they are the *universal set*, written $\mathscr{E}$. At other times we will be referring to a set of file cards. They form a different universal set. Any universal set is written as $\mathscr{E}$.

We use { } to enclose the elements of a set and a capital letter, when convenient, to name it. For instance, $Z = \{$Alan Amber, Bessie Black, Charles Crimson$\}$ means the set Z whose elements are the three children named.

If $Y = \{$the first three children on the list$\}$, what can you say about Z and Y? They are said to be *equal*. Sets are called equal if they have the same elements. We write $Z = Y$.

The set Z was specified by listing its elements. The set Y was specified by giving a description of its elements. Either method can be used, but for some sets listing is virtually impossible, for instance $\{$children in the world today$\}$.

Some sets are actually impossible to list completely, for instance $\{$fractions$\}$. Why is this? Name another *infinite set*.

We use the symbol $\in$ to mean 'belongs to' and $\notin$ to mean 'does not belong to'. Charles Crimson $\in Z$ but Kitty Khaki $\notin Z$.

2. COMPLEMENTARY SETS

Sometimes the school secretary needs to find out quickly which children take school dinners, or come to school on their cycles. One way of doing this is to make a file card for each child. For example, a card with four holes punched along the top could be used. A card is prepared for each child and the whole set is kept in a box. They are sorted by pushing a thin knitting needle through one or more of the holes and lifting out the cards which are not required. A typical card is shown in Figure 1.

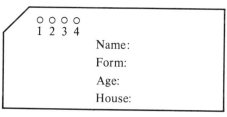

Figure 1

The secretary uses the four holes of the card to code the yes/no information in the last four columns of the form lists. Figure 2 shows the card for Alan Amber. The card is clipped away above holes 1 and 4 because there is the word 'Yes' in the corresponding columns on the list. Holes 2 and 3 are left intact because they correspond to the word 'No' on the list.

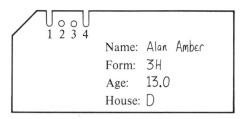

Figure 2

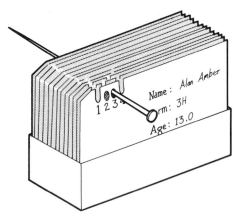

Figure 3

When the secretary has made a card for each child she puts them in a box as in Figure 3, all facing the same way. She pokes a knitting needle through (say) the third holes of all the cards, shakes it to release any cards not hooked, and lifts the hooked ones out of the box. Will Alan Amber's card still be in the box? Why not? Which cards will be left? From now on we shall write a for Alan Amber's card, b for Bessie Black's card and so on. Notice that now $\mathscr{E} = \{\text{file cards}\} = \{a, b, \dots, o\}$.

The cards left in the box will be $C = \{d, k, m, o\}$. Check this from the form list. What do the corresponding children have in common? The cards that have been lifted from the box form the *complementary set*. We write C' for this complementary set. If $D = \{\text{cards of children taking school dinner}\}$, check that $D' = \{d, j\}$.

3. INTERSECTION OF SETS

The secretary keeps the set C (for cyclists) in the box and removes a second set of cards by pushing her knitting needle through the fourth holes, corresponding to the set D. The cards remaining in the box belong to both set C and set D. We call this set the *intersection* of sets C and D and write it $C \cap D$.
$$C = \{d, k, m, o\} \quad D = \{a, b, c, e, f, g, h, i, k, l, m, n, o\} \quad C \cap D = \{k, m, o\}$$

Suppose now that the secretary returns all the cards to the box and carries out the same procedure with sets C and B (for bus users). What will happen now? The set $B \cap C$ has no members. We call it the *empty set*. It can be written either as $\{\ \}$ or as $\varnothing$.

4. UNION OF SETS

The secretary now puts all the cards back in the box. She puts a needle through the third holes as before and a second needle through the fourth holes. She gives the cards a shake and lifts. What set will be left in the box?

(a)   (b)

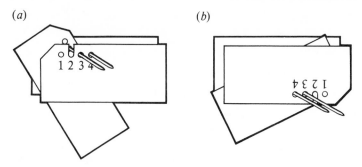

Figure 4

She keeps hold of the two needles and holds them horizontally. Some of the cards are supported by the two needles and are horizontal. Some are supported by only one and, one way up or the other, they will tip sideways as shown in Figure 4. She separates these and puts them back in the box, removing only the ones that were hooked on both needles. The cards in the box will belong to C or D (or both). We call this the *union* of sets C and D and write it $C \cup D$.

List the members of $C \cup D$. Which set of cards has been removed from the box? Describe it in symbols.

Exercise A

You may like to prepare a set of cards before you start this exercise. You can either make them for our imaginary children, as listed on p. 54, or for members of your own form. All the questions refer to

$\mathscr{E} = \{\text{cards of children listed in 3H}\}$,
$A = \{\text{cards of children who live more than 4 km away}\}$,
$B = \{\text{cards of children who travel to school by bus}\}$,
$C = \{\text{cards of children who cycle to school}\}$,
$D = \{\text{cards of children taking school dinners}\}$.

1 List the sets A, B, C and D and keep the lists for reference when answering the questions in this exercise and Exercise B.

*2 Write in words:
  (a) $A \cup B$;   (b) $A \cap B$.

3 Write in words:
  (a) $A \cap D$;   (b) $A \cup D$.

*4 Express in terms of A, B, C and D:
  (a) the set of cards of children who travel to school by bus or take school dinners (or both);
  (b) the set of cards of children who cycle to school and take school dinners.

5 Write in set language:
  (a) cards of children who do not travel to school by bus;
  (b) cards of children who do not travel to school by bus and live more than 4 km from school.

*6 List the members of the sets:
  (a) $A \cup D$;   (b) $B \cap C$.
  What other sets are these equal to?

7   List the elements of the sets:
    (a) $A' \cup B'$;   (b) $A' \cap B'$.

*8   Write in words:
    (a) A';   (b) C'.

9   Write in words:
    (a) B';   (b) $A \cup B'$.

*10   Are the following statements true or false?
    (a) $A \cap B = B \cap A$;   (b) $B' \cup A = A \cup B'$.

11   List the elements of the sets:
    (a) $A \cap B$;   (b) $(A \cap B) \cap D$;   (c) $B \cap D$;   (d) $A \cap (B \cap D)$.
    What do you find? Do you think this would be true for any three sets?

12   List the members of:
    (a) $A \cup C$;   (b) $(A \cup C) \cup D$;   (c) $C \cup D$;   (d) $A \cup (C \cup D)$.
    What do you find? Do you think this would be true for any three sets?

5. VENN DIAGRAMS

Figure 5 shows a Venn diagram. It is named after the English mathematician who wrote about this way of making a drawing of sets. The sets A and B are represented by closed curves and the universal set by the rectangle enclosing them. The curves representing A and B overlap to show that there are elements which belong to both A and B; $A \cap B \neq \varnothing$. It does not matter what shape the curves are, or whether they are large or small.

Sometimes it is useful to write the actual elements in the appropriate regions as in Figure 6, but usually it is just the overall impression of how the sets relate that is needed.

Shading can be used to indicate a particular set. Figure 7 shows the set $A \cap B$.

What can you say of the sets in Figure 8? Are any of the sets A, B, C, D in this relation to each other?

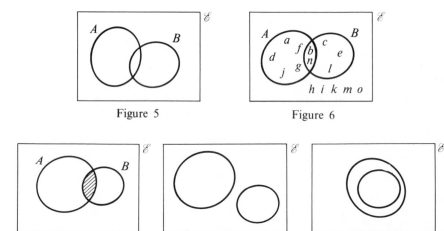

Figure 5

Figure 6

Figure 7

Figure 8

Figure 9

What can you say of the sets in Figure 9? Are any of the sets A, B, C, D in this relation to each other?

6. SUBSETS

If $P = \{b, e, n\}$ then P is called a *subset* of $B = \{b, c, e, l, n\}$ since every element of P is also an element of B. We write $P \subseteq B$. What will $Q \not\subseteq B$ mean? What will $B \supseteq P$ mean?

The number of elements in the set P is 3, and we write $n(P) = 3$. What is $n(B)$? What is the relation between $n(J)$ and $n(B)$ if $J \subseteq B$?.

There is one subset of B (and only one) that has 5 elements. It is B itself. Explain how the definition of a subset requires that $B \subseteq B$. Every set, then, is a subset of itself. The other subsets are called *proper subsets*. $\varnothing$ is regarded as a proper subset of every set.

Exercise B

(This exercise refers to A, B, C, D and $\mathscr{E}$ as defined at the beginning of Exercise A.)

*1   (a) List the sets B and C and show them in a Venn diagram.
     (b) What are: (i) $n(B)$; (ii) $n(C)$; (iii) $n(B \cup C)$?
 2   (a) List the sets A and C and show them in a Venn diagram.
     (b) What are: (i) $n(A)$; (ii) $n(A \cup C)$; (iii) $n(A \cap C)$?
*3   Draw a Venn diagram showing the sets B and D, writing in the elements as in Figure 6.
 4   Draw a Venn diagram showing the sets C and D, writing in the elements in the appropriate regions.
*5   Write $n(A), n(B), n(C)$ and $n(D)$ in order, with the smallest number first.
 6   Write $n(A'), n(B'), n(C')$ and $n(D')$ in order, with the smallest number first.
*7   What are:
         (a) $n(\mathscr{E})$;   (b) $n(A \cup A')$;   (c) $n(B \cup B')$?
 8   What are:
         (a) $n(\varnothing)$;   (b) $n(C \cap C')$;   (c) $n(D \cap D')$?
*9   Draw a Venn diagram showing the sets A, B and C, writing in the elements in the appropriate regions.
10   Draw a Venn diagram showing the sets A, C and D, writing in the elements in the appropriate regions.

7. ANOTHER NOTATION

Especially when dealing with sets of mathematical objects, it is useful to have a shorthand for specifying sets. We use a colon to mean 'such that' and write, for example, $F = \{x : x > 1\}$ for 'F is the set of numbers x such that x is greater than 1'. If $\mathscr{E} = \{\text{whole numbers}\}$ then $F = \{2, 3, 4, 5, \ldots\}$, but if $\mathscr{E} = \{\text{real numbers}\}$ then F contains numbers such as $1.0001, 1.37$ and 9.86421.

This notation is mostly used for sets of numbers or sets of pairs of numbers, but it is also used for sets of points, as we shall see in the next chapter.

When $\mathscr{E} = \{\text{real numbers}\}$ a set such as F can be represented on a number line, as in Figure 10. Notice the small circle which shows that $1 \notin F$.

Figure 10. $F = \{x : x > 1\}$.

Figure 11 shows $G = \{x : x \leqslant 4\}$. Notice how the fact that $4 \in G$ is shown in the diagram.

Figure 11. $G = \{x : x \leqslant 4\}$.

Figures 12 and 13 show $F \cap G$ and $F' \cup G'$. Notice the different ways in which these can be written.

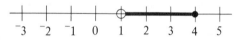

Figure 12. $F \cap G = \{x : x > 1\} \cap \{x : x \leqslant 4\} = \{x : x > 1 \text{ and } x \leqslant 4\} = \{x : 1 < x \leqslant 4\}$.

Figure 13. $F' \cup G' = \{x : x \leqslant 1\} \cup \{x : x > 4\} = \{x : x \leqslant 1 \text{ or } x > 4\}$.

All of the sets above are infinite sets. But if $\mathscr{E} = \{\text{whole numbers}\}$, what is $F \cap G$?

Exercise C

In questions 1–8, $\mathscr{E} = \{\text{real numbers}\}$.
*1   If $H = \{x : x > {}^-1\}$ and $K = \{x : x < 3\}$, represent H, K and $H \cap K$ on number lines.

2   If $L = \{x : x \geqslant 4\}$ and $M = \{x : x < 5\}$, represent L, M and $L \cap M$ on number lines.

*3   If $P = \{x : x < 0\}$ and $Q = \{x : x \geqslant 3\}$, represent P, Q, and $P \cup Q$ on number lines.

4   If $R = \{x : x \leqslant {}^-2\}$ and $S = \{x : x > 2\}$, represent R, S and $R \cup S$ on number lines.

*5   If $T = \{x : {}^-1 \leqslant x < 2\}$, represent T on a number line.

6   If $V = \{x : 0 < x \leqslant 5\}$, represent V on a number line.

*7   If $W = \{x : x < \frac{1}{2} \text{ or } x > 1\}$, represent W on a number line.

8   If $X = \{x : x \leqslant 0 \text{ or } x > 2\}$, represent X on a number line.

*9   If $\mathscr{E} = \{\text{whole numbers}\}$, list the following sets:
     $Y = \{n : 1 \leqslant n < 5\}$; $Z = \{n : n > 1 \text{ and } n^2 < 10\}$.

10   If $\mathscr{E} = \{\text{whole numbers}\}$, list the following sets:
     $Y = \{p : p \text{ is prime and } p^2 < 100\}$; $Z = \{q : q \text{ is even and } 5q \leqslant 43\}$.

SUMMARY

'Set' is the word for a collection of objects. A set is specified by listing or by giving a rule which enables us to decide whether an object belongs to it or not. A member of a set is also called an element of the set.

A set with an infinite number of elements is called an infinite set.

$a \in A$ means that a is an element of the set A.

The complete set of things we are considering is called a universal set, written $\mathscr{E}$.   (Section 1)

Given $\mathscr{E}$ and a set A within $\mathscr{E}$, the complementary set, A', consists of the elements of $\mathscr{E}$ which are not elements of A.   (Section 2)

If C and D are sets then the set of elements belonging to both C and D is called the intersection of C and D, written $C \cap D$.   (Section 3)

The set of elements belonging to C or D or both is called the union of C and D, written $C \cup D$.   (Section 4)

Sets and the relationships between them can be illustrated by Venn diagrams.   (Section 5)

The number of elements in a set A is written $n(A)$.

If every element of A also belongs to B then A is a subset of B, written $A \subseteq B$.

If $A \subseteq B$ and $n(A) < n(B)$ then A is a proper subset of B.   (Section 6)

$\{x : \ldots\}$ means 'the set of x such that ...'   (Section 7)

Summary exercise

In questions 1–3,
$\mathscr{E} = \{\text{whole numbers less than } 20\}$,
$M = \{\text{multiples of } 3\}$,
$V = \{\text{multiples of } 5\}$,
$S = \{\text{multiples of } 6\}$.

1   List the elements of the following sets:
    (a) M;   (b) V;   (c) S;   (d) $M \cap V$;   (e) $V \cup S$.

2   Draw a Venn diagram to illustrate the sets M, V and S. Write the numbers 1 to 19 in the appropriate regions of your diagram.

3   State whether the following statements are true or false. If a statement is false, give a correct version.
    (a) $M \subseteq S$;   (b) $n(M \cap V) = 2$;   (c) $M' \cap S = \varnothing$;   (d) $n(V \cup S) > n(M)$.

4   Show $A \cap B$ on a number line if $\mathscr{E} = \{\text{real numbers}\}$, $A = \{x : x \geqslant {}^{-}1\}$ and $B = \{x : x < 3\}$.

Miscellaneous exercise

1   If $\mathscr{E} = \{\text{first eight letters of the alphabet}\}$, $P = \{f, a, c, e\}$ and $Q = \{b, a, c, h\}$,
    (a) list the members of (i) $P \cap Q$; (ii) $P' \cup Q'$;
    (b) draw a Venn diagram to illustrate P and Q, writing in all eight elements of $\mathscr{E}$ in their appropriate regions;
    (c) what is the relation between $P \cap Q$ and $P' \cup Q'$?

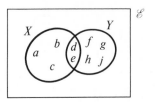

Figure 14

2   With $\mathscr{E}$, P and Q defined as in question 1, list the members of (i) $P' \cap Q'$ and (ii) $(P \cup Q)'$ and state the relation between them.

3   If sets X and Y are related as shown in Figure 14, write down $n(X)$, $n(Y)$, $n(X \cap Y)$ and $n(X \cup Y)$. Can you see a simple relation between these numbers?

4   In a group of 10 students, 7 learn French and 4 learn German. Draw Venn diagrams for the various possibilities and hence find all four possible answers to the question 'How many students learn both?'

5   With $\mathscr{E}$, P and Q defined as in question 1 and $R = \{h, e, a, d\}$,
    (a) draw a Venn diagram to illustrate P, Q and R, writing in all eight elements of $\mathscr{E}$ in their appropriate regions;
    (b) for each of the eight regions of your diagram, list the corresponding members and describe the set in terms of P or P', Q or Q', R or R' and the symbol $\cap$. (For example, $\{c\} = P \cap Q \cap R'$.)

6   Make two copies of the Venn diagram in Figure 15 and shade $(P \cup Q) \cap R$ on one and $(P \cap R) \cup (Q \cap R)$ on the other. What do you notice?

7   Make a copy of the Venn diagram in Figure 15 and use different shadings to show the sets $P \cup R$ and $Q \cup R$. Can you write $(P \cup R) \cap (Q \cup R)$ in a simpler form?

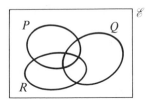

Figure 15

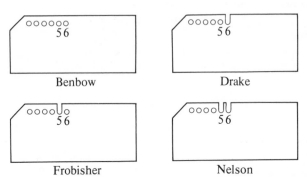

Figure 16

8 If Z is any set, simplify:

(a) $Z \cup \varnothing$; (b) $Z \cap \varnothing$; (c) $Z \cup \mathscr{E}$; (d) $Z \cap \mathscr{E}$.

9 If Z is any set, simplify:

(a) $Z \cup Z'$; (b) $Z \cap Z'$.

10 Referring back to the start of this chapter you may have been wondering how the secretary could code the cards to pick out children of different houses and different ages. This is how she copes with different houses. She gives each house a binary number: Benbow 00; Drake 01; Frobisher 10; Nelson 11. Then she uses two new holes as shown in Figure 16.

  (a) Which cards will be left in the box if she puts her needle through the fifth holes and lifts?

  (b) How would she get cards for children in Frobisher only?

  (c) How does she get cards for children in Nelson?

Discuss how a similar method could be used to pick out the cards of children with different ages. How many holes will be required?

6

Loci

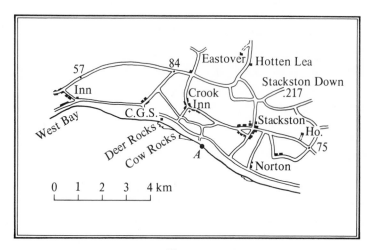

Figure 1

1. LOCUS

Figure 1 shows a coastal region of the Isle of Sampsey. A boat-owner hires out boats from a boat-station, near Cow Rocks, marked *A*. Draw a similar coastline and mark a boat-station. Rowing-boats may not be taken more than 1 km from the shore. Draw the boundary and shade the region where rowing-boats are permitted. Sailing-boats may not be taken more than 3 km from *A*. Use a geometrical instrument to draw the new boundary line and shade in a different way the region where sailing-boats are permitted.

Your freehand drawing of the 1 km line and the circular arc representing a distance of 3 km from *A* (did you use compasses?) are both examples of what mathematicians call a *locus*. They are sets of points satisfying a clearly stated condition, such as being 1 km from another line, or 3 km from a point.

Each region that you shaded is also an example of a locus. What conditions do points in them satisfy?

Locus is a Latin word meaning place or position. Its plural is *loci*.

Figure 2 shows an unfortunate situation. A window-cleaner is standing two-thirds of the way up a ladder. The ladder slips down the wall and the window-cleaner clings on to the ladder. Is his locus a straight line? Or a curve? Describe what you think happens.

To find out what happens we draw two lines at right angles to each other to

64

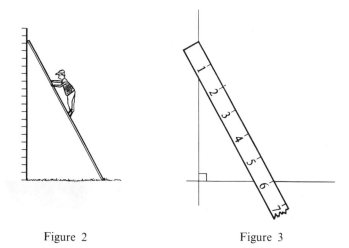

Figure 2   Figure 3

represent the walls, and another line of fixed length, say 6 cm, to represent the ladder. Since the window-cleaner is two-thirds of the way up we will represent him by a dot 2 cm from the top. It is simplest to use the edge of your ruler as in Figure 3. Put it in about ten different positions, each time marking where the dot comes on the paper. Be careful to keep the 0 and 6 cm marks on the lines.

What we have done is called *making a mathematical model* of a physical situation. It *simulates* the real-life situation less painfully but still enables us to answer the question: 'what is the locus of the window-cleaner as he falls?'

The set of all positions of the window-cleaner in space and the set of all the black dots that you marked (and all those you could have marked) are two further examples of loci.

Exercise A

*1   Figure 4 shows the back garden of a house. The owner decides to plant an apple tree in the garden. It must be at least 6 m from the house and at least 5 m from the trunk

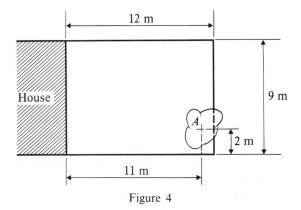

Figure 4

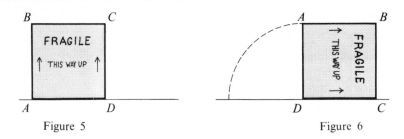

Figure 5   Figure 6

of the existing tree, A. Draw the diagram to scale and show the possible positions where he can plant the tree

2 (*a*) A square-ended box is being rolled across the floor without slipping. Figure 5 shows the starting position. First of all the box rotates about the corner D, and this causes the point A to move on a circular path as shown in Figure 6. With the help of compasses, draw the locus of A from the position shown in Figure 5 until A is on the floor again.

(*b*) Repeat part (*a*) with a rectangular-ended box.

(*c*) Repeat part (*a*) with a box whose ends are equilateral triangles (like a Toblerone chocolate box).

*3 A bicycle is being ridden at a steady speed in a straight line. Write down a description of the locus of (*a*) the bell; (*b*) the centre of the front wheel; (*c*) a point on the outer rim of a tyre; (*d*) the endpoint of the spindle of a pedal. (It may help you to carry out a simulation as in question 2 by drawing a number of positions, or by using a coin.)

4 The locus of points at which television reception from a certain type of transmitter is satisfactory is the interior of a circle of radius about 50 km. Trace Figure 7 and draw in the locus of points having satisfactory reception if the transmitters are at the point A, B and C.

If only two transmitters are available, at which two of these points should they be placed in order to obtain the greatest coverage of land? Is this the main consideration in practice? Discuss the merits of the possible schemes.

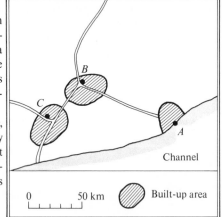

Figure 7

*5 Figure 8 shows Patricia (P) learning to become a trapeze artiste. Trapeze A and trapeze B will come together at C and she will change from the one to the other. Draw a mathematical model of the locus of her hands before and after the exchange.

6 Figure 9 shows the window-cleaner again. This time the leg A breaks off his ladder, but B stays on the ground. What is his locus this time?

7 Say which of the following loci are straight lines, which curved lines and which are

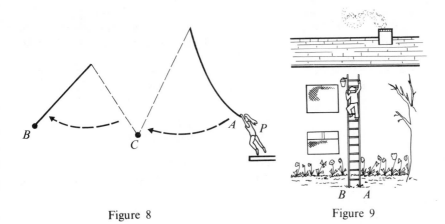

Figure 8   Figure 9

regions. Which would be very difficult to represent on a piece of paper? Why?

(a) Points on the shortest path from the top right-hand corner to the bottom left-hand corner of this page;

(b) points 2 cm from the top left-hand corner of this page;

(c) points further from the centre of London than from the centre of Edinburgh;

(d) the path traced by the nose of a woman standing on an escalator;

(e) the path traced by the nose of a man walking up a spiral staircase;

(f) points inside an inflated spherical balloon.

8   Figure 10 shows (i) part of a line p, (ii) part of a half-line q and (iii) a line segment AB. Copy the figure and sketch the locus of a point which is always 2 cm from (a) the line p; (b) the half-line q; (c) the line segment AB.

(i)   (ii)   (iii)

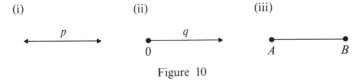

Figure 10

***9**   In Figure 11, A and B are fixed points 5 cm apart and P is a variable point. The area of triangle APB is 10 cm^2. Find the distance from P to AB. Draw the locus of P. (It has two distinct parts.)

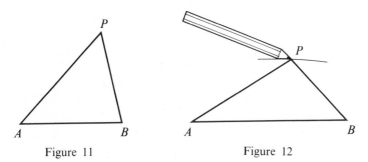

Figure 11   Figure 12

10 In Figure 12, *A* and *B* are fixed 10 cm part and the perimeter of the triangle is 28 cm. Draw the locus of *P*. This can be easily done by making a loop of string 28 cm long and looping it around two drawing pins at *A* and *B*. A pencil, as shown, keeps the loop taut and draws the locus of *P*.

You will find that the locus is an oval curve called an ellipse. This is the curve you see if you shut one eye and look at a circle whose plane is not at right-angles to your line of sight. Describe its symmetries.

2. LOCUS AND SET NOTATION

It is sometimes useful to use set notation to describe loci. Figure 13 shows the section of coast referred to at the beginning of the chapter, together with the sets *R* and *S*, where

$\mathscr{E} = \{$points on the surface of the sea$\}$,
$R = \{$permitted positions for rowing boats$\}$
$\quad = \{P : P$ is less than 1 km from the shore$\}$,
$S = \{$permitted positions for sailing boats$\}$
$\quad = \{P : PA < 3$ km$\}$.

This last statement is read as '*S* is the set of points *P* such that *PA* is less than 3 km'.

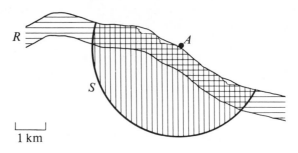

Figure 13

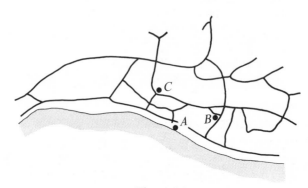

Figure 14

The boat-owner is told that one of his rowing-boats collided with one of his sailing-boats and an oar was lost overboard. Where would he start looking for the oar? The collision must have occurred at a point which was in both region R and S, i.e. at a point of $R \cap S$, so this is the region in which he should start his search.

$R \cup S$ is the region in which all his boats (rowing or sailing) should be, so this is the region he would have to patrol if he wanted to warn those who had hired his boats of an impending storm, or that he was about to shut his boat-station.

Exercise B

*1   Figure 14 shows the road network in this area of the Isle of Sampsey and the Crook Inn (C) and the Bosun's Arms, Stackston (B). Trace Figure 14 and use your copy of the map to answer the following questions:

    (a) A is equidistant from B and C (i.e. $AB = AC$). Find two T-junctions which are equidistant from B and C and label them T_1 and T_2 on your map.

    (b) A gull leaves the boat-station at A and flies inland in such a way that it is always equidistant from B and C. Draw its route on the map.

    (c) If $\mathscr{E} = \{$points (P) on the Isle of Sampsey$\}$, use set notation to describe the points on the ground immediately under the gull's line of flight.

    (d) The landlord of the Bosun's Arms put up posters (advertising a darts match) at the three crossroads which are nearer the Bosun's Arms than the Crook Inn. Label these crossroads X_1, X_2 and X_3 on your map.

    (e) Shade the set $\{X : XB < XC\}$ on your map. Are X_1, X_2 and X_3 members of this set?

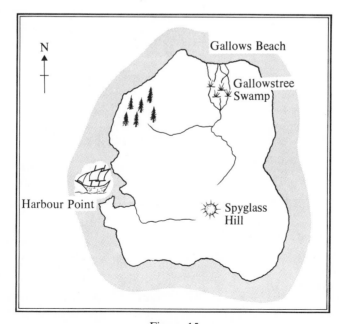

Figure 15

2 Draw a line segment AB of length 6 cm. Construct the locus $\{P : PA = PB\}$.

*3 Draw a line segment AB of length 8 cm. Construct the loci $R = \{P : PA = 6 \text{ cm}\}$ and $S = \{P : PB = 5 \text{ cm}\}$. Show clearly the set $R \cap S$.

4 Draw a line segment XY of length 7 cm. Construct the locus $\{P : PX > PY\}$.

*5 Draw a line segment XY of length 6 cm. Construct the locus $\{P : PX < 5 \text{ cm}\}$. Is Y an element of this set?

6 Figure 15 shows a sketch map of Silicon Island. Spyglass Hill is 8 km south of Gallows Beach and 6 km east of Harbour Point. Under questioning Little Charlie Digger reveals the following clues about where the Magic Chip is buried:

(1) the case is buried 1 m deep and 6 km from Gallows Beach;

(2) it is in a leather case 5 km from the Harbour Point;

(3) the burial place is nearer Spyglass Hill than Gallows Beach.

(*a*) Write the conditions (1)–(3) in set notation.

(*b*) Draw an accurate diagram to find where the Magic Chip is buried. How far is the burial place from Spyglass Hill?

3. USE OF COORDINATES

Many loci can be conveniently described using a coordinate system. Cartesian coordinates give the distances x and y of a point from the two axes, as shown in Figure 16.

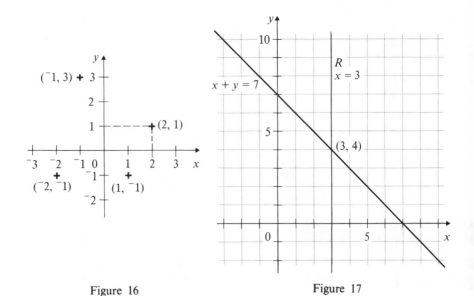

Figure 16   Figure 17

The locus $R = \{(x, y) : x = 3\}$ contains points with coordinates such as $(3, 1), (3, 2), (3, 5), (3, \frac{1}{2}), (3, 0.9), (3, 0), (3, {}^-1)$ and so on. It is shown in Figure 17.

The locus $S = \{(x, y) : x + y = 7\}$ contains points with coordinates such as $(7, 0), (6, 1), (3, 4), (2.7, 4.3), (0, 7), ({}^-1, 8), ({}^-5, 12)$ and so on. $R \cap S$ is a single point with coordinates $(3, 4)$.

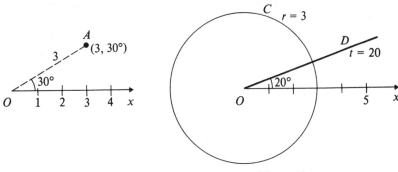

Figure 18   Figure 19

Polar coordinates give the distance r from the origin and the angle $t°$ between OA and the initial line: in Figure 18 the point A has polar coordinates $(3, 30°)$ since OA is 3 units and the angle xOA is 30°. (The initial line is usually taken across the page; the angle is measured anti-clockwise.)

The locus $C = \{(r, t°):r = 3\}$ consists of all the points 3 units from the origin and is a circle. The locus $D = \{(r, t°):t = 20\}$ is shown together with C in Figure 19.

Exercise C

*1 On the same diagram, draw the following loci:
$A = \{(x, y):x = 5\}$, $B = \{(x, y):y = 2\}$ and $C = \{(x, y):x = 1\}$.
Give the coordinates of the points belonging to
(a) $A \cap B$; (b) $A \cap C$.

2 On the same diagram, draw the following loci:
$P = \{(x, y):y = 1\tfrac{1}{2}\}$, $Q = \{(x, y):y = 4\}$ and $R = \{(x, y):x = 2\tfrac{1}{2}\}$.
List the elements of $(P \cup Q) \cap R$.

*3 Write down the coordinates of five points on the locus $\{(x, y):y = x\}$ and show the locus on a diagram.

4 Write down the coordinates of five points on the locus $\{(x, y):x + y = 3\}$ and show the locus on a diagram.

*5 If $Q = \{(x, y):x > 3\}$ and $R = \{(x, y):y < 5\}$, show Q, R and $Q \cap R$ on three separate diagrams.

6 If $S = \{(x, y):x < 5\}$ and $T = \{(x, y):y > {}^-1\}$, show S, T and $S \cap T$ on three separate diagrams.

*7 With Q, R, S and T as defined in questions 5 and 6, show the following sets on separate diagrams:
(a) $Q \cap S$; (b) $R \cap T$; (c) $Q \cup T$; (d) $Q \cap R \cap S \cap T$.

8 With Q, R, S and T as defined in questions 5 and 6, show the following sets on separate diagrams:
(a) Q'; (b) $Q' \cup S'$; (c) $(Q' \cup S') \cap R$; (d) $(Q' \cup S') \cap R \cap T$.

*9 On the same diagram, draw the following loci:
$A = \{(r, t°):r = 4\}$, $B = \{(r, t°):t = 90°\}$.

10 On the same diagram, draw the following loci:
$R = \{(r, t°):r = 5\}$, $S = \{(r, t°):t = 130\}$.

*11   If $A = \{(r, t^\circ) : r > 3\}$ and $B = \{(r, t^\circ) : r < 6\}$, show A, B and $A \cap B$ on three separate diagrams.

12   If $C = \{(r, t^\circ) : t > 20\}$ and $D = \{(r, t^\circ) : t < 110\}$, show $C \cap D$ on a diagram.

*13   If $R = \{(r, t^\circ) : r < 3\}$ and $S = \{(r, t^\circ) : t = 45\}$, show $R \cap S$ on a diagram.

14   Use set notation and polar coordinates to describe the following loci shown in Figure 20:
  (a) the circle radius 2 units;
  (b) the line segment OR;
  (c) the semi-circular region shaded.

*15   Figure 21 shows a photographer's lamp L and a screen which has the shape of a 90°

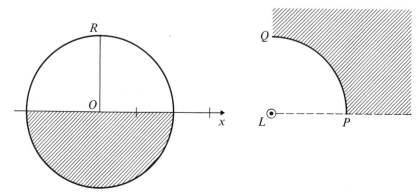

Figure 20   Figure 21

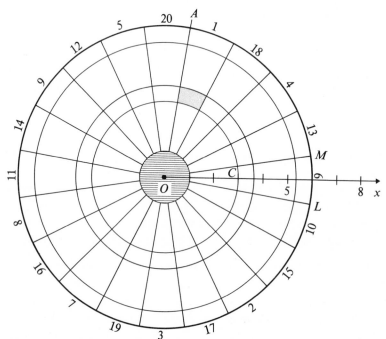

Figure 22

arc, *PQ*, of a circle of radius 3 m. Describe the locus of a point in the shaded region using polar coordinates and taking the line *LP* as central direction.

16 Figure 22 illustrates a dartboard. The numbers round the circumference are the scores that a player obtains if he hits the regions labelled. Take *Ox* as initial line and use polar coordinates, with the scale indicated. (The outer circle is of radius 6 units.)

    (*a*) Calculate the angles
        (i) *MOL*;   (ii) *MOx*;   (iii) *AOx*.
    (*b*) Describe the circle centre *O* through *C*.
    (*c*) Describe the region (a sector of the outer circle) marked 20.
    (*d*) Describe the central shaded region.
    (*e*) Describe the region for '*treble* 1' (shown stippled).
    (*f*) Describe the 'double' region which lies between the two outer circles.

4. LINKAGES

Linkages are often used in everyday objects. One of the simplest possible linkages is a pair of compasses. Reclining chairs and some pedal bins use more complicated linkages. Work through the following investigations.

(*a*) You will need two strips of card the same length and also a strip about twice as long.

Arrange the strips as shown in Figure 23. They are fixed to the board at *A* and *B* with drawing-pins. The strips are linked at *C* and *D* with drawing-pins, points uppermost.

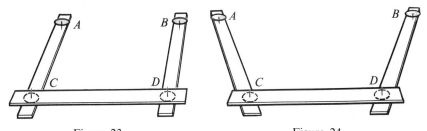

Figure 23   Figure 24

    (i) Make a hole in the middle of *CD* and put a pencil point through it. Move the strips so that *CD* stays parallel to *AB*. What is the locus of the pencil point?

        Try the pencil point in another hole which is not in the middle of *CD*.

    (ii) Move the drawing-pins at *A* and *B* so that the distance between them is greater than *CD* (see Figure 24). Put the pencil point through the middle of *CD* and find its locus.

        Try the pencil in other holes also.

(*b*) Take two strips, not necessarily equal in length. Pin one end of each to a board and make holes at the other ends. Bring these ends together and put a pencil point through them. Try to move the pencil around. What do you find?

Figure 25

Exercise D

In this exercise hinged joints are shown like this:

fixed joints like this:

hinged points, fixed in space, like this:

or this

*1 Figure 26 represents a windscreen wiper, *EFG* being the blade. *D* and *A* are fixed to the top of the windscreen. What are the loci of *B*, *C*, *F* and *E* as the angle *t* varies? What is the purpose of this linkage?

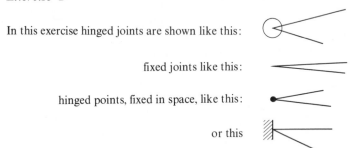
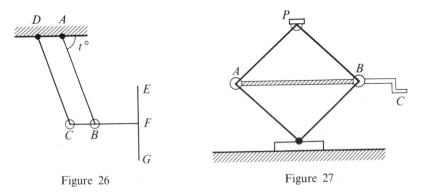

Figure 26   Figure 27

  2 Figure 27 shows a type of car jack. As the handle *C* is turned *A* and *B* are pulled closer together by the screw thread. What is the locus of *P*? Why does this enable you to lift a heavy weight?

*3 Figure 28 shows a pair of 'lazy tongs'. What happens to the jaws *M* and *N* as the handles *A* and *B* are brought together? Describe the loci of *T*, *U*, *M* and *N* assuming that *A* and *B* move together along a fixed vertical line. Why are they called 'lazy tongs'?

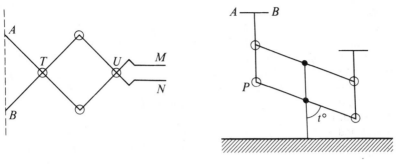

Figure 28   Figure 29

4   Figure 29 represents a letter balance. What are the loci of P and of A and B, as t varies? Why is the balance made like this? (There are two reasons, one more difficult to understand than the other!)

5   Figure 30 is a diagram of Watt's Linkage. P is the midpoint of BC and A, P, D start in a straight line. What do you think will be the locus of P as t is varied? Make a model and verify your guess. You should find that two portions of the locus are fairly straight, and can be made more so by varying the lengths of the strips. It was this property that James Watt made use of in his steam engines. (See Figure 25.)

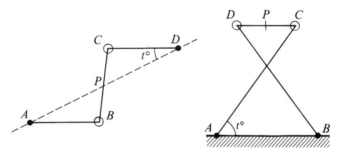

Figure 30   Figure 31

6   Figure 31 is a diagram of Tchebychef's linkage. Guess the locus of P as t varies. Make a model and verify your guess. It is necessary for the lengths to be in the proper ratio for this to work properly. A suitable set of lengths are: $AC = BD = 10$ cm, $AB = 8$ cm, $CD = 4$ cm. P is the midpoint of CD; AC and BD can slide freely past each other.

*7 Figure 32 shows a pantograph, a machine used for enlarging geometrical figures.

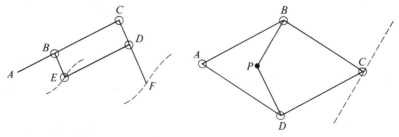

Figure 32   Figure 33

BCDE is a parallelogram and *A, E, F* are in a straight line. *E* and *F* are drilled so that a pencil point or ball point refill can be poked through. If *E* is made to follow a diagram, *F* will trace an enlargement of it. What will be the scale factor? How can the machine be used for reducing? It is possible to buy a pantograph, but try to make your own. Decide on a scale factor first and make one to fit.

8 (*Project*) Figure 33 is a diagram of Peaucellier's Cell. *ABCD* is a rhombus and *BP* = *PD*. *A* and *C* are drilled so that a pencil point or a ballpoint refill can be poked through. If *C* is made to follow a straight line, *A* will trace a curve. Make a model (some care is needed) and try to identify the curve. What happens if *A* is made to follow a straight line? Add an extra link *PA* = *PD* and repeat the experiment.

5. USEFUL CONSTRUCTIONS

Mediator of two points

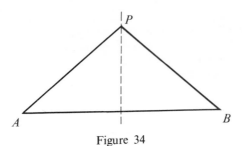

Figure 34

(1) Mark two points *A* and *B* about 10 cm apart on a piece of tracing paper. Join them up by a line. Fold the tracing paper so that *A* maps onto *B*. What can be said about the fold line and the line *AB*? Take any point *P* on the fold line. Join it to *A* and *B*. (See Figure 34.) What can be said about the lengths of *PA* and *PB*? If in doubt fold the paper again so that *A* maps onto *B*.

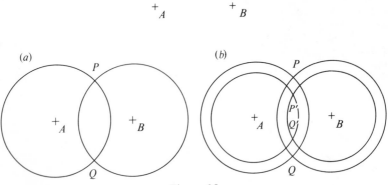

Figure 35

(2) Spike the mathematical spider has to walk across the paper so that his distance from *A* is always the same as his distance from *B* (Figure 35).

Describe his locus. It is called the *mediator* of the points A, B, or the *perpendicular bisector* of AB.

(3) It is not convenient to be continually folding pages to find the mediator of two points. So we look for another method, one that uses drawing instead. In Figure 35(*a*) a circle has been drawn with centre A and another with the same radius, with centre B. The radius has been chosen so that the circles cut at two convenient points P and Q. Why is $PA = PB$? Why is $QA = QB$? In Figure 35(*b*) another pair of equal circles has been drawn. What can you say about $P'A$ and $P'B$? What can you say about P', P, Q and Q'? They are points of a locus. Write it down in set notation.

Mediator of two lines

(1) Draw a larger version of Figure 36 on tracing paper. Fold your tracing paper so that line 1 maps onto line 2.

    Take any point on your fold line and join it at right-angles to each line as shown in Figure 37. What can be said about the lengths of PM and PN?

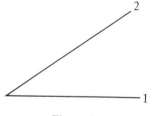

Figure 36

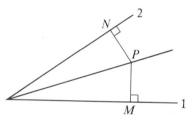

Figure 37

(2) Spike has to walk across the paper so that his distance from line 1 is always the same as his distance from line 2. Describe his locus. It is called the *mediator* of lines 1 and 2, or the *bisector* of the angle between 1 and 2.

(3) In Figure 38 an arc of a circle has been drawn to cut the lines 1 and 2 at Q and R. With centres Q and R two equal arcs have been drawn to cut at Y. What can you say about the symmetry of the figure as a whole? What relation will the line OY have to the lines 1 and 2? If P is any point on OY write down a description of the line in set notation.

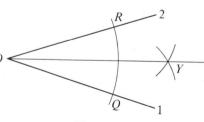

Figure 38

Exercise E

1 Draw a triangle ABC with $AB = 10$ cm, $BC = 9$ cm and $CA = 7$ cm. Use the method illustrated in Figure 38 to draw the bisectors of the three angles. What do you find?

Draw another triangle *DEF* of a different size and shape from *ABC*. Repeat the construction. Comment on what you find.

2 Draw a triangle *ABC* with *AB* = 9.5 cm, *BC* = 11.5 cm and *CA* = 8 cm. Use the method illustrated in Figure 35 to draw the perpendicular bisectors of the sides *AB, BC, CA*. What do you find? Draw another triangle *DEF* of different size and shape from *ABC*. Repeat the construction. Comment on what you find.

3 Three boys lit a firework and immediately ran off in different directions at the same speed. Figure 39 show where they were when it exploded. Where did the firework go off?

   We can argue like this. Since Alan and Bob ran at the same speed for the same length of time they must be equidistant from the explosion. Draw the mediator of *A* and *B*. The explosion must lie on this line. Why? The same thing is true about Bob and Charlie. Draw another mediator and solve the problem.

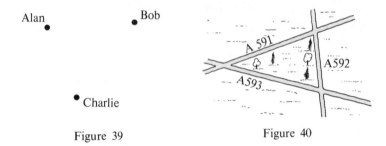

Figure 39   Figure 40

4 Figure 40 shows three busy main roads surrounding a common. A caravaner wishes to put his caravan on the common but as far as possible from each road. Use your answer to question 1 to help him find the best site.

*5 In a triangle *ABC* the mediator of *A* and *B* cuts the mediator of *B* and *C* at *F*. (See Figure 41.)

   (*a*) What can you say about
      (i) the lengths *FA* and *FB*;
      (ii) the lengths *FB* and *FC*?
   (*b*) What can you deduce about *FA* and *FC*?
   (*c*) What does this tell you about the relationship between *F* and the mediator of *A* and *C*?
   (*d*) What do your answers to (*a*) and (*b*) tell you about the circle centre *F* radius *FA*?

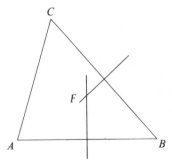

Figure 41

6 The point which is the same distance from each of the three vertices of a triangle is called its *circumcentre*. Is it possible for a circumcentre to lie outside its triangle?

If so, construct one. Draw the circle through each of the vertices. This is called the circumcircle.

7 Draw two lines AB and CD cutting at O. (See Figure 42) Draw the bisectors of the angles AOC, COB and DOA. What do you find? Why is it ambiguous to talk about *the* mediator of the lines AB and CD?

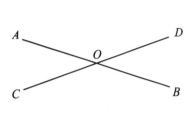

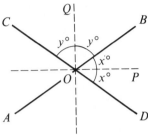

Figure 42   Figure 43

8 *Interior and exterior bisectors of an angle*
Figure 43 shows the lines AB and CD cutting O. OP bisects $\angle BOD$, so $\angle BOP$ and $\angle DOP$ have both been marked x. Similarly $\angle BOQ$ and $\angle COQ$ have both been marked y. What can you say about $x + x + y + y$? What can you say, therefore, about $x + y$? What does this tell you about the lines OP and OQ?

*9 Draw a triangle ABC in which $AB > AC$. Construct accurately the locus of a point P such that its distance from AB is greater than its distance from AC. Take $\mathscr{E} = \{$points inside triangle $ABC\}$.

10 The point at which the three angle bisectors of a triangle meet is called its *in-centre*. Is it possible for an in-centre to lie outside its triangle? If so, draw one.

11 Draw the triangle ABC in which $AB = 8.7$ cm, $BC = 6.9$ cm and $\angle ABC = 75°$. Construct its in-centre. (The word *construct* means that you must use the method of $(b)(3)$ above, not merely measure angles.) Call this I. Draw the perpendicular ID from I to the side BC. With centre I and radius ID draw a circle (called the in-circle). What do you find? Account for what you find.

12 Use a method similar to that of question 5 to explain carefully *why* the three angle bisectors of a triangle meet at the point that we call the in-centre.

6. LOCI IN THREE DIMENSIONS

Figure 44 shows two tower blocks each with a light on the top. A helicopter pilot landing on the helipad at night is told to fly between the buildings and keep equidistant from the lights. What will be his path? It is not possible to say whether it will be a straight line or a curve. What is certain is that the flight path will be in the *mediator plane* of the two lights.

Previously in this chapter we have assumed that loci lie in a plane, usually the plane of a piece of paper or blackboard. Now we consider loci in space.

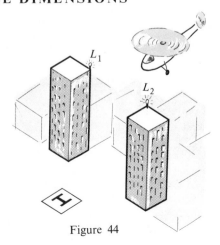

Figure 44

Exercise F

*1 (*a*) Describe the set of possible positions of a model aircraft on a taut control line 30 m long fastened to a fixed point on level ground.

(*b*) Describe the locus of the same model aircraft if it is flying at a height of 10 m.

2 If O is a fixed point in space describe in words the loci

(*a*) $\{P:OP = 3\}$;   (*b*) $\{P:OP > 3\}$;   (*c*) $\{P:OP \leqslant 3\}$.

*3 If $\mathscr{E} = \{$ points in space $\}$, describe the locus of a point 3 m away from:

(*a*) a line l;   (*b*) a line segment AB.

4 Hold up a piece of paper. What is the locus of a point which is always 2 cm from the paper?

*5 Use set notation to describe the locus of a point on earth in the northern hemisphere.

6 Figure 45 represents the label from a cocoa tin. Sketch the path, in space, of Freda the mathematical fly if she crawls from A to C when the label is on the tin. Name some familiar objects that possess this shape.

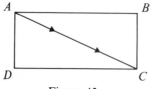

Figure 45

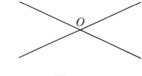

Figure 46

*7 Two straight horizontal wires in space cut at O as shown in Figure 46. What is the locus of a point equidistant from the two lines?

8 Let $X = \{P:P$ is 4 cm from a plane $\pi\}$ and $Y = \{P:P$ is 5 cm from A, where A is a fixed point in $\pi\}$.

Describe (*a*) X;   (*b*) Y;   (*c*) $X \cap Y$.

9 Let l be a line in a plane π. If $X = \{P:P$ is 2 cm from $\pi\}$, and $Y = \{P:P$ is 3 cm from $l\}$, describe $X \cap Y$.

10 Let π be the infinite plane of which your paper is a part. If c is a line perpendicular to π and $X = \{P:P$ is 10 cm from $c\}$, identify X and $\pi \cap X$.

Sketch $\pi \cap X$ if c makes an acute angle with π.

SUMMARY

A locus is a set of points satisfying some condition, which may be specified either geometrically or algebraically.

A locus can be a line, a curve, a region or one or more individual points.

(Sections 1, 2, 3)

Loci can occur in two or three dimensions and so the universal set of points should be specified. (Section 6)

A linkage is a hinged set of rods used for a variety of practical purposes.

(Section 4)

For the mediator (perpendicular bisector) of two points, A, B:

Draw two arcs of equal radius, centres at the points. Join their intersections (Figure 47).

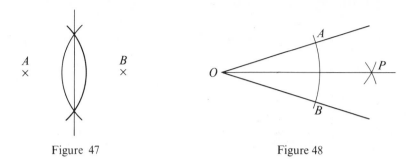

Figure 47   Figure 48

For the mediator (bisector) of the angle between two lines:
Draw an arc, centre at the vertex O of the angle, to cut both arms, at A and B.
With these points as centres draw two arcs of equal circles to cut each other.
Join their intersection to the vertex of the angle (Figure 48).   (Section 5)

Summary exercise

1   Roll a 5p piece round another 5p piece as shown in Figure 49. Mark points and so
     construct the locus of a point on the rim of the moving 5p piece. The figure is called
     a *cardioid*. (Why?)
2   Draw a circle of radius 3 cm and the locus of a point 3 cm from this circle. (Take care,
     you may not have the whole locus!)
3   If $\mathscr{E} = \{$ points on your page$\}$ and A, B, C are three points in a straight line such that
     $AB = 4$ cm and $BC = 6$ cm, (Figure 50), construct and label the following sets:
     (*a*) (i) $L = \{P : AP < 2\,\mathrm{cm}\}$;
           (ii) $M = \{P : BP < 7$ cm$\}$;
          (iii) $N = \{P : BP = CP\}$.
     (*b*) $L \cap M$. Write down a relation between L and M.
     (*c*) $L \cap N$. Write down a relation between L and N.

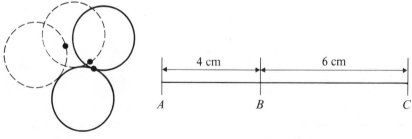

Figure 49   Figure 50

4   Draw the isosceles triangle ABC in which $AB = AC = 8.5$ cm and $BC = 6.6$ cm.
     Construct the locus of points within the triangle nearer to AB than to BC.
5   On squared paper construct the sets
     $J = \{(x, y) : x = 2y\} \cap \{(x, y) : x \leqslant 4\}$ and $K = \{(x, y) : y \geqslant {}^{-}1\} \cap \{(x, y) : y \leqslant 2\}$.
\6   Figure 51 shows the regions getting good, satisfactory and poor reception from a
     local radio station at O. The thick line represents a range of hills cutting off all reception

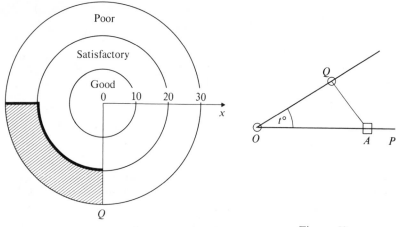

Figure 51   Figure 52

in the shaded area. Taking Ox as initial line and with the scale shown write down expressions in polar coordinates for the three circles, the line segment OQ and the shaded area.

7   Identify the common object in which the linkage shown in Figure 52 is used and explain what happens as the slider A moves along the rod OP, and t varies.

8   Construct the triangle PQR in which $\angle P = 72°$, $\angle Q = 84°$, $PQ = 5$ cm. Construct the interior bisector of $\angle R$ and the exterior bisectors of $\angle P$ and $\angle Q$. Comment on what you find. Is there a circle associated with what you find? If so, what does it do?

9   A and B are two points in space 6 cm apart, P is such that $PA = 4$ cm and $PB = 5$ cm. What is the locus of P?

10   If A and B are fixed points in space, describe the following loci:
   (a) $\{P : AP = 1 \text{ cm}\}$;   (b) $\{P : AP < BP\}$.

Miscellaneous exercise

1   Draw two circles, centres P and Q, such that their radii are 3 cm and 2 cm respectively and $PQ = 7$ cm. By measurement find a number of positions of a point which is the same distance from the circle centre P as it is from the circle centre Q. Hence sketch its locus and try to identify its shape.

2   Spike the spider walks on the surface of a cube of edge 10 cm from one vertex to the diametrically opposite vertex. What is the shortest distance that he can walk? (Hint: find his locus on the net of the cube.)

3   (a) Draw two points P and P' and construct a point X not on PP' such that P can be mapped into P' by a rotation about X.
   (b) The line segment QR is to be mapped onto the equal line segment $Q'R'$, Q onto Q' and R onto R', by a rotation about a point Y. Copy Figure 53, making the angles roughly the same and the lengths about twice as great and construct the point Y as accurately as you can. (Make your construction clear. If you do it by folding the paper, pencil in the folds.) If J is the point where QR cuts $Q'R'$ what can you say about the relation of Y to the angle QJR'?

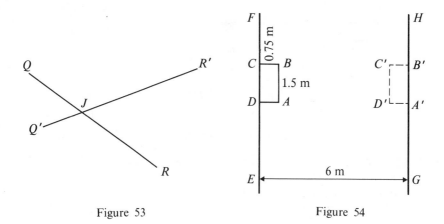

Figure 53   Figure 54

(c) Two lines l and l' meet at K. S is a point on l and S' is a point on l' such that $KS \neq KS'$. The line l is rotated onto l' so that S maps onto S'. Describe clearly with the aid of a sketch how you can find the two possible centres of rotation V and W.

4   In Figure 54 the rectangle $ABCD$ represents a heavy piano measuring 1.5 m by 0.75 m. It is to be moved from its present position against the wall EF of a hall to the opposite wall GH. The method is to rotate it through 30° clockwise about its corner A and then through 30° anti-clockwise about its corner B. Similar rotations are then made, though not necessarily about the same corners.

Copy the diagram on a larger scale. Show the locus of each corner during one pair of rotations. Hence find whether it will be possible to move it to its new position $A'B'C'D'$ without any transformations other than the rotations mentioned.

5   Copy the two rectangles shown in Figure 55 and construct accurately a centre of rotation for the first onto the second. Can you find more than one such centre? If so, how many? Add them to your diagram in a different colour.

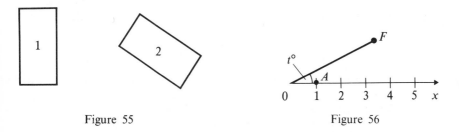

Figure 55   Figure 56

6   An aircraft which never runs out of fuel starts at a place on the equator. The pilot flies in a steady direction 045°. Describe his locus and say where he finishes up.

7   A, B, C are three points in space. Describe the locus $\{P : AP = BP = CP\}$. D is a fourth point, not in the plane ABC. Describe the locus $\{P : BP = CP = DP\}$ and give reasons why the two loci intersect. What is the relation between this point of intersection and A, B, C, D?

8   Freda (F) the mathematical fly starts at A in Figure 56 and walks on the paper so that her locus is $\{(r, t°) : r = \frac{1}{10}t + 1\}$. Copy the diagram on a larger scale and mark her position at intervals of 10° from 0° to 50°; hence sketch her path.

7

Equations

1. EQUATIONS

I think of a number, double it, add three and my result is nineteen. What number did I think of?

In algebraic notation we can write this as:
$$2x + 3 = 19, \quad \text{find } x.$$

I start again with a different number and my result is 5.6 after doubling and adding three. Can you discover what I thought of now?

You will probably have managed this too. But you may like to remind yourself of the principles to be sure of success.

Example 1

Solve

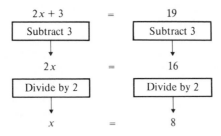

The flow chart shows how we convert $2x + 3$ into x. It merely reverses the stages of doubling and adding three. The same process converts 19 into 8.

Exercise A

*1 (*a*) I think of a number, double it, add five and my result is thirteen. What number did I think of?

   (*b*) Solve the equations: (i) $2x + 5 = 13$; (ii) $2y + 5 = 19$.

2 (*a*) I think of a number, multiply it by three, add two and my result is seventeen. What number did I think of?

   (*b*) Solve the equations: (i) $3t + 2 = 17$; (ii) $3v + 2 = 26$.

*3 (*a*) Five tonnes of seed potatoes were delivered to Hank's farm. The total bill, including a 7-dollar delivery charge, was 242 dollars. What was the cost of a tonne of seed potatoes?

   (*b*) Solve the equations: (i) $5c + 7 = 132$; (ii) $5c + 7 = 42$.

4 (*a*) Car-parking charges in the Westditch car-park are 40p for the first hour and 10p for each subsequent hour. On my last visit I had to pay 90p. For how many hours did I park?

   (*b*) Solve the equations: (i) $30 + 10q = 90$; (ii) $30 + 10r = 130$.

*5   Solve the equations:
     (a) $4a + 7 = 19$;   (b) $3b + 5 = 23$;   (c) $2c - 5 = 11$;   (d) $3d - 7 = 22$.

6   Solve the equations:
     (a) $5a + 2 = 17$;   (b) $3b + 11 = 35$;   (c) $5c - 8 = 27$;   (d) $7d - 2 = 33$.

*7   Solve the equations:
     (a) $2w + 3 = 10$;   (b) $3x + 5 = 12$;   (c) $5y - 3 = 13$;   (d) $7z - 6 = 11$.

8   Solve the equations:
     (a) $5p + 8 = 19$;   (b) $4q + 3 = 9$;   (c) $3r - 7 = 13$;   (d) $6s - 5 = 23$.

*9   (a) I think of a number, add five, double my answer and the result is sixteen. What number did I think of?
     (b) Solve the equations: (i) $2(x + 5) = 16$;   (ii) $2(y + 5) = 26$.

10   (a) I think of a number, subtract five, multiply the answer by three and the result is eighteen. What number did I think of?
     (b) Solve the equations: (i) $3(x - 5) = 18$;   (ii) $3(y - 5) = 36$.

*11   Solve the equations:
     (a) $2(p + 7) = 19$;   (b) $3(q + 2) = 21$;
     (c) $5(r - 2) = 45$;   (d) $6(s - 4) = 30$.

12   Solve the equations:
     (a) $2(w + 11) = 38$;   (b) $8(x + 13) = 248$;
     (c) $3(y - 7) = 39$;   (d) $7(z - 11) = 84$.

2. REVERSE FLOW

For more complicated equations you may need to consider carefully how an algebraic expression is built up.

Example 2

Solve the equation $\dfrac{3x - 4}{5} = 7$.

The function $f : x \longrightarrow \dfrac{3x - 4}{5}$ corresponds to the flow chart

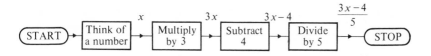

To find x we need to reverse the flow chart as follows:

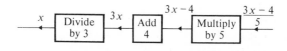

We can therefore solve the equation using the same steps.

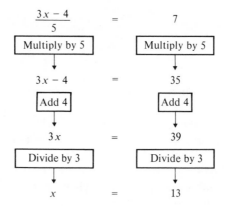

Since we are always using the same operation on both sides of the equation, we shall not, in future examples, repeat the instruction.

Example 3

Solve the equation $\dfrac{24}{y} - 1 = 7$.

The function $y \longrightarrow \dfrac{24}{y} - 1$ corresponds to the flow chart containing the following instructions:

$$y \rightarrow \boxed{\text{Find the reciprocal}} \xrightarrow{\frac{1}{y}} \boxed{\text{Multiply by 24}} \xrightarrow{\frac{24}{y}} \boxed{\text{Subtract 1}} \xrightarrow{\frac{24}{y}-1}$$

(In order to concentrate attention on the operations and their order we have omitted the START and STOP and incorporated the arrows into the rectangular instruction boxes.)

The reverse flow chart has the following instructions:

$$y \leftarrow \boxed{\text{Find the reciprocal}} \xleftarrow{\frac{1}{y}} \boxed{\text{Divide by 24}} \xleftarrow{\frac{24}{y}} \boxed{\text{Add 1}} \xleftarrow{\frac{24}{y}-1}$$

So we solve the equation by using the same operations, like this:

$$\frac{24}{y} - 1 = 7$$

Add 1

$$\frac{24}{y} = 8$$

Divide by 24

$$\frac{1}{y} = \frac{8}{24} = \frac{1}{3}$$

Find the reciprocal

$$y = 3$$

Exercise B

Solve these equations, using reversed flow charts if necessary.

*1   (a) $\dfrac{2x+1}{3} = 5$;   (b) $\dfrac{3y-1}{4} = 8$.

2   (a) $\frac{1}{2}(5x-7) = 4$;   (b) $\frac{1}{3}(4y+1) = 7$.

*3   (a) $11 - 2z = 5$;   (b) $16 - 3t = 4$.

4   (a) $3(7-p) = 15$;   (b) $2(9-q) = 28$.

*5   (a) $\frac{2}{3}(m+7) = 8$;   (b) $\frac{3}{4}(n-11) = 15$.

6   (a) $\frac{2}{5}(2x-3) = 6$;   (b) $\frac{4}{7}(4y-1) = 20$.

*7   (a) $\dfrac{6}{z} = 3$;   (b) $\dfrac{12}{w-2} = 4$.

8   (a) $3 + \dfrac{12}{u} = 5$;   (b) $\dfrac{12}{3+v} = 5$.

*9   (a) $\dfrac{5}{w+3} = \dfrac{1}{2}$;   (b) $\dfrac{4}{x-5} = \dfrac{2}{3}$.

10   (a) $\dfrac{36}{2x+1} = 4$;   (b) $\dfrac{24}{3y-2} = 6$.

3. SIMPLIFICATION

Using reversed flow charts is only appropriate if the unknown appears just once in an equation. But sometimes it may be possible to simplify an equation, using the distributive law, until it satisfies this condition.

Example 4

Solve the equation $5x - 9 + 2x = 6 + 3x$.

Collect together

$$7x - 9 = 6 + 3x$$

Subtract $3x$ from both sides

$$4x - 9 = 6$$

Add 9

$$4x = 15$$

Divide by 4

$$x = \frac{15}{4}$$

Check: if $x = \dfrac{15}{4}$ the left hand side of the equation $=$

$$5x - 9 + 2x = \frac{75}{4} - \frac{36}{4} + \frac{30}{4} = \frac{69}{4}$$

and the right hand side $= \quad 6 + 3x = \dfrac{24}{4} + \dfrac{45}{4} = \dfrac{69}{4}$

Example 5
  Solve the equation $\quad 3(x - 5) - 2(2x - 3) = 8$

Write the equation without brackets
$$3x - 15 - 4x + 6 = 8$$
Collect together
$$^-x - 9 = 8$$
Add 9
$$^-x = 17$$
Change sign
$$x = {}^- 17$$

Check: $x = {}^-17 \Rightarrow 3(x - 5) - 2(2x - 3) = 3(^-22) - 2(^-34 - 3)$
$$= {}^-66 - 2(^-37) = {}^-66 + 74 = 8$$

Exercise C

*1   Solve the following equations:
  (a) $5x + 2 = 2x + 11$;   (b) $3y + 7 = y + 17$;
  (c) $8a = a - 14$;   (d) $2p = 3p + 6$.
2   Solve the following equations:
  (a) $8h + 9 = 21 - 4h$;   (b) $6n - 7 = 17 - 2n$;
  (c) $40 - 3m = 2m - 35$;   (d) $3 - 2q = 5q + 31$.
*3   Solve the following equations:
  (a) $3(x + 5) + x = 23$;   (b) $2(y - 7) = y - 6$;
  (c) $4(5 - u) = 3u - 1$;   (d) $5(2v - 3) + 3v = 11$.
4   Solve the following equations:
  (a) $2(3 - p) - 3(4 - p) = 7$;   (b) $5(q - 7) = 4(7 - q)$;
  (c) $3(2r + 1) - 2(5 - 2r) = 13$; (d) $7(s - 5) - 6(4 - s) = 6$.

4. PROBLEM-SOLVING

Example 6
  A journey of 300 km is partly through built-up areas and partly on a motorway. A driver's average speed through the built-up areas is 40 km/h and on the motorway is 90 km/h. For how many hours did she drive on the motorway if the complete journey took 4 hours?

If we write t for the number of hours of motorway driving, then she averaged 90 km/h for t hours and 40 km/h for $(4 - t)$ hours; during these times she drove $90t$ km and $40(4 - t)$ km. But the total distance was 300 km.

$$90t + 40(4 - t) = 300$$
$$90t + 160 - 40t = 300$$
$$50t + 160 = 300$$
$$50t = 140$$
$$t = \frac{140}{50} = \frac{14}{5}$$

So she drove for $2\frac{4}{5}$ hours or 2 hours 48 minutes on the motorway.

Check: 90 km/h for $2\frac{4}{5}$ hours: distance travelled $= 252$ km
        40 km/h for $1\frac{1}{5}$ hours: distance travelled $= 48$ km
        Total distance travelled $= 300$ km

Example 7

Thirty coins (5-pence and 10-pence pieces) are fed into a coin-box to pay for a £1.75 telephone call. How many of the coins were 10-pence pieces?

If n is the number of 10-pence coins, then the value of the 10-pence coins is $10n$ pence, the number of 5-pence coins is $30 - n$, and their value is $5(30 - n)$ pence.

The total value of the coins is $10n + 5(30 - n)$ pence.

Hence $10n + 5(30 - n) = 175$
                       $10n + 150 - 5n = 175$
                              $5n = 25$
                              $n = 5.$

There were five 10-pence coins.

Check: Five 10-pence coins are worth 50 pence $\left.\right\}$ Total value £1.75
        Twenty-five 5-pence coins are worth £1.25 $\left.\right\}$

Notice that all the quantities must be in the same units: pence, in this case.

Exercise D

*1 Tickets for a concert cost 60p or 80p. The number of 80p tickets sold was 200 less than the number of 60p tickets sold. The total of the ticket sales was £680. The number of 60p tickets sold was n.
  (*a*) Write down expressions involving n for:
      (i) the number of 80p tickets sold;
      (ii) the total cost of the 60p tickets sold;
      (iii) the total cost of the 80p tickets sold.
  (*b*) Write down an equation for n and solve it.
  (*c*) How many tickets were sold altogether?

2 In a multiple-choice test 3 marks are given for a correct answer and one mark is subtracted for each incorrect answer. A candidate answers fourteen questions, x of them correctly.
  (*a*) How many questions did she answer incorrectly?
  (*b*) How many marks did she obtain for her correct answers?

(c) How many marks did she lose for her incorrect answers?

(d) If her total mark was 22, write down an equation for x and solve it.

*3 Peter rows upstream at 5 km/h for z minutes and then rows downstream to his starting-point at 10 km/h. He takes 63 minutes altogether.

(a) Write down expressions involving z for:

    (i) the distance he rows upstream;

    (ii) the time for which he rows downstream;

    (iii) the distance he rows downstream.

(b) Write down an equation for z and solve it.

(c) How far upstream did Peter row?

4 Jane's father is four times her age, and her mother is three years younger than him.

(a) If Jane is q years old, write down expressions involving q for:

    (i) her father's age;

    (ii) her mother's age.

(b) When the ages of Jane and her parents are added together, the total is 96. Write down an equation for q and solve it.

(c) How old is Jane's mother?

*5 A bottle of cider costs 48p. The cider costs 36p more than the bottle. Find the cost of the bottle.

6 Fifty 2p and 5p coins have a value of £1.96. How many of the coins are 2p pieces?

*7 A shopkeeper bought some tea at £4 per kilogram and mixed it with twice as much tea of a cheaper variety at £3 per kilogram. He sold all the mixture at £5 per kilogram, making a profit of £20. How many kilograms of tea did he sell altogether?

8 Tom is three times as old as his son Harry. In twelve years time Tom will be twice as old as Harry will be then. How old is Harry now?

5. INEQUALITIES

We now investigate whether it is possible to use the same methods that we have used for equations to solve inequalities.

Exercise E

*1 Figure 1 shows the set $S = \{x : x > 3\}$.

Draw similar diagrams to illustrate the following sets:

$A = \{2x : x \in S\}$,

$B = \{x + 2 : x \in S\}$,

$C = \{x - 2 : x \in S\}$,

$D = \{^-x : x \in S\}$,

$E = \{^-2x : x \in S\}$.

State whether it is true or false that if $x > 3$, then

(a) $2x > 6$;   (b) $x + 2 > 5$;   (c) $x - 2 < 1$;   (d) $^-x > ^-3$;   (e) $^-2x < ^-6$.

2 State whether the following statements are true or false:
  (a) If $3y > 12$ then $y > 4$.
  (b) If $t + 7 > 19$ then $t < 12$.
  (c) If $z > {}^-5$ then $-z < 5$.
  (d) If ${}^-3v > 12$ then $v > {}^-4$.

*3 If $S = \{3,\ 3.1,\ 3\frac{1}{2},\ 3.7,\ 4, 5,\ 100\}$, list the members of S which satisfy each of the following inequalities:
  (a) $x \geqslant 4$; (b) $2x < 7$; (c) $7 - x \leqslant 3$; (d) $10 - 2x < 0$.

Solving inequalities

We can obtain an equivalent inequality by adding or subtracting the same number to both sides, or by multiplying or dividing both sides by the same positive number. If both sides are multiplied or divided by a negative number, then the inequality is reversed. For example, the inequalities $x > 3$ and ${}^-2x < {}^-6$ are equivalent.

Example 8
  Solve the inequalities:
  (a) $\dfrac{3x - 4}{5} \geqslant 7$; (b) $3(2 - x) + x < 7$.

(a) Multiply by 5
$$3x - 4 \geqslant 35$$
  Add 4
$$3x \geqslant 39$$
  Divide by 3
$$x \geqslant 13$$

(b) Write without brackets
$$6 - 3x + x < 7$$
  Collect together
$$6 - 2x < 7$$
  Subtract 6
$$-2x < 1$$
  Divide by -2
$$x > -\tfrac{1}{2}$$

Exercise F

Solve the following inequalities.
*1 $2x + 5 > 13$.
*3 $2(x - 1) \leqslant 12$.
*5 $3 - 4x < 27$.
*7 $33 - 2x > x + 18$.
*9 $\frac{1}{2}(3x - 1) > 10$.

2 $3t + 7 \geqslant 25$.
4 $3(x + 3) < 15$.
6 $5 - 2x \geqslant 17$.
8 $7 - 3x \geqslant 2x - 8$.
10 $\frac{2}{3}(4x + 7) < 8$.

6. TRANSPOSITION OF FORMULAE

The speed, v m/s, of a wave of frequency f hertz (Hz) and wavelength λ m is given by the formula $v = f\lambda$. Radio waves travel at 3.0×10^8 m/s. The wavelength of BBC Radio 4 is 1500 m; what is the frequency of its transmission?

Writing 3.0×10^8 for v and 1500 for λ we have

$$3.0 \times 10^8 = f \times 1500$$
$$f = \frac{3.0 \times 10^8}{1500} = 2.0 \times 10^5.$$

The frequency of Radio 4 is therefore 2.0×10^5 Hz, or 200 kHz.

The wavelength of Radio 1 is 275 m; what is its frequency?

If we are carrying out a series of calculations of this kind it would be useful to have a formula for f in terms of v and λ, i.e. to have f as the *subject* of the formula. In the same way as we solve the equation above we can deduce that

$$v = f\lambda \quad \Leftrightarrow \quad f = \frac{v}{\lambda} \quad \text{(by dividing both sides of the equation by } \lambda\text{).}$$

For Radio 1, $f = \dfrac{3.0 \times 10^8}{275} \approx 1.1 \times 10^6$; the frequency is 1100 kHz, approximately.

Example 9

Make t the subject of the formula $v = u + at$.

$$v = u + at \quad \Leftrightarrow \quad v - u = at \qquad \text{(subtracting } u\text{)}$$
$$\Leftrightarrow \quad \frac{v - u}{a} = t \qquad \text{(dividing by } a\text{)}$$
$$\Leftrightarrow \quad t = \frac{v - u}{a}$$

Exercise G

*1 A stone is dropped down a well. Its speed, v m/s, t seconds later is given by the formula $v = 10t$.
   (a) Find t when $v = 15$.
   (b) Make t the subject of the formula.
   (c) Find t when (i) $v = 25$;   (ii) $v = 22$;   (iii) $v = 37$.

2 The power P watts consumed by an appliance is given by the formula $P = VI$, where V volts is the potential difference and I amperes (A) is the current flowing.
   (a) Find I when $P = 1000$ and $V = 250$.
   (b) Make I the subject of the formula.
   (c) Find the current through
       (i) a 3000-watt kettle connected to a 240-volt supply;
       (ii) a 180-watt television connected to a 240-volt supply;
       (iii) a 500-watt hair-dryer connected to a 110-volt supply;
       (iv) a 500-watt hair-dryer connected to a 240-volt supply;

(v) an electric cooker rated at 13 200 watts (with the oven and all the rings full on) connected to a 240-volt supply.

(d) Fuses are available at ratings of 2, 5 and 13 A. (For example, a 2-amp fuse will burn out if the current through it exceeds 2 A). Which fuses would be appropriate for the kettle, television and hair-dryer connected to a 240-volt supply?

*3 The potential difference V volts across a resistor with resistance R ohms is given by the formula $V = IR$, where I amperes is the current flowing through the resistor.

(a) Find R when $V = 110$ and $I = 2$.

(b) Make R the subject of the formula.

(c) Find the resistance of
   (i) a kettle which uses a current of 12 A when connected to a 240-volt supply;
   (ii) a light-bulb which uses a current of $\frac{1}{4}$ A from a 240-volt supply;
   (iii) a television which uses a current of $\frac{2}{3}$ A from a 120-volt supply;
   (iv) an immersion heater which uses a current of 15 A from a 240-volt supply.

4 The Fahrenheit and Celsius scales of temperature are related by the formula:
$$y = \tfrac{9}{5}x + 32$$
where $y°$F and $x°$C represent the same temperature.

(a) Find x when $y = 50$.

(b) Make x the subject of the formula.

(c) Find the Celsius measurements corresponding to:
   (i) 68°F;   (ii) 212°F;   (iii) normal body temperature, 98.4°F;
   (iv) 136°F, a shade temperature recorded in the Sahara;
   (v) ⁻34°F, an average July temperature in Antarctica.

*5 A train is slowing down in such a way that t seconds after its brakes were applied its speed, v m/s, is given by the formula:
$$v = 60 - \tfrac{1}{2}t.$$

(a) How many seconds of braking reduce its speed to 48 m/s?

(b) Make t the subject of the formula.

(c) (i) After how many seconds is the train travelling at 24 m/s?
   (ii) How long does it make the train to stop?

6 Using the formula $v = f\lambda$ where v m/s = velocity of wave
$$f\ \text{Hz} = \text{frequency}$$
$$\lambda\ \text{m}\ = \text{wavelength}$$

(a) find the wavelength of the soundwave in air of concert A (440 Hz) given that the velocity of sound in air is 330 m/s;

(b) make λ the subject of the formula;

(c) find the wavelengths of:
   (i) E above middle C (330 Hz);
   (ii) Cadmium blue light: frequency 6.25×10^{14} Hz (velocity of light is 3.0×10^8 m/s);
   (iii) a VHF radio signal of 90 MHz (MHz is the abbreviation for megahertz; 1 MHz $= 10^6$ Hz; velocity of radio waves $\approx 3.0 \times 10^8$ m/s).

*7 Make x the subject of each of the following formulae:

(a) $y = 3x - 2$;   (b) $y = 2(x + 5)$;   (c) $v = ax + b$;

(d) $z = \dfrac{3}{2 + x}$;   (e) $t = \dfrac{a}{a + x}$;   (f) $s = \dfrac{x + a}{x}$.

SUMMARY

An equation can be solved by applying the same operations to both sides to obtain the unknown quantity.   (Section 1)

Reversing a flow chart can be used to decide what operations to apply to both sides.   (Section 2)

If the unknown letter occurs more than once in an equation, the distributive law can be used to simplify the equation by collecting together appropriate terms and writing expressions without brackets.   (Section 3)

Inequalities can be solved by similar methods to those used for solving equations, but multiplying or dividing by a negative number reverses an inequality.   (Section 4)

Techniques similar to those used for solving equations can be used to re-arrange formulae.   (Section 5)

Summary exercise

1   Solve the following equations:
   (a) $3x + 7 = 11$;   (b) $\frac{1}{3}(x + 7) = 11$;

   (c) $16 - 5x = 31$;   (d) $\dfrac{24}{x + 3} = 3$.

2   Bill runs 6 km/h faster than he walks. If he runs for $\frac{1}{2}$ hour and walks for $\frac{3}{4}$ hour he covers 10 km. How fast does he run?

3   Solve the equations:
   (a) $3(x - 2) - 2(4 - x) = 6$;   (b) $3(y + 4) = 5y - 8$.

4   Solve the inequalities:
   (a) $\frac{1}{4}(3x + 7) > 1$;   (b) $3(4 - 5x) + 2(3 - x) \geqslant 8$.

5   The density, ρ kg/m^3, of a substance is given by the formula $\rho = \dfrac{m}{V}$, where m kg is the mass of a volume of V m^3 of the substance.
   (a) A gold coin has a mass of 0.031 kg and a volume of 1.6×10^{-6} m^3. Find its density.
   (b) Silver has density 10.5×10^3 kg/m^3. Find the mass of a silver coin of volume 1.6×10^{-6} m^3.
   (c) Make V the subject of the formula and use your answer to find:
      (i) the volume occupied by 1 kg of air of density 1.29 kg/m^3;
      (ii) the volume of a 1-tonne ingot of steel of density 7.8×10^3 kg/m^3.

Miscellaneous exercise

1   Solve the following equations:
   (a) $2x^2 - 5 = 7 - x^2$;   (b) $\dfrac{12}{y^2 - 5} = 3$;   (c) $\dfrac{18}{5 - z^3} + 6 = 0$.

2   Two cars travel from Sampsey to Umbridge at average speeds of 50 km/h and 60 km/h. If they start at the same time and the slower car arrives $\frac{3}{4}$ hour after the faster one, how far is it from Sampsey to Umbridge?

3 Thirty-six people paid a total of £165 in fares on the Sampsey to Umbridge coach. The adult fare is £5 and the child fare is £2.50. How many fare-paying children were there on the coach?

4 One morning Ruth sets out walking at 1.5 m/s to the station 1 km away but finishes by running at 5 m/s. Find how far she ran if she took 8 minutes altogether.

5 A train normally runs over a stretch of d kilometres at a speed of v km/h. On one occasion it enters the stretch m minutes late, but by running at u km/h it arrives at the end of the stretch at the correct time.

(a) Show that $d = \dfrac{m}{60} \Big/ \left(\dfrac{1}{v} - \dfrac{1}{u} \right)$.

(b) Find u when $v = 90$, $m = 2$ and $d = 30$.

6 (a) Copy and complete the following table:

x	$^-4$	$^-3$	$^-2$	$^-1$	$^-\frac{1}{2}$	$\frac{1}{2}$	1	2	3	4	6
$\dfrac{1}{x}$					$^-2$						
$\dfrac{12}{x}$										4	

(b) Solve the following inequalities, using your answers to (a) as a check:

(i) $\dfrac{1}{x} > \dfrac{1}{2}$; (ii) $\dfrac{1}{x} < \dfrac{1}{2}$; (iii) $\dfrac{12}{x} > 4$; (iv) $\dfrac{12}{x} < 4$; (v) $\dfrac{12}{x} < {}^-4$.

(c) Show the sets $A = \left\{ x : \dfrac{1}{x} \geq \dfrac{1}{2} \right\}$ and $B = \left\{ x : \dfrac{1}{x} < \dfrac{1}{2} \right\}$ on a number line. What is the relation between A and B?

REVISION EXERCISE 5

1   Write in standard form:

(a) 301 030;   (b) $2 \times 10^{-6} \times 6 \times 10^4$,   (c) $\dfrac{1}{10\,000}$;   (d) $\dfrac{1}{0.0005}$.

2   Find $f(2)$ for each of the following functions:

(a) $f : x \longrightarrow 3(x - 7)$;   (b) $f : x \longrightarrow \frac{1}{3}x^2 - 7$;

(c) $f : x \longrightarrow \dfrac{6}{x} + 3x$;   (d) $f : x \longrightarrow \dfrac{3}{x - 5}$.

3   Estimate to an accuracy of one significant figure:

(a) the cost of 394 noglets at 31p each;

(b) the cost of petrol for a journey of 513 km for a car which uses 8.3 litres of petrol every 100 km, if petrol costs 47p per litre.

4   Write down:

(a) the number of seconds in z hours;

(b) the number of minutes taken to travel d km at a steady speed of q km/h.

5   If $x = 4$, $y = 2$ and $z = 3$,   find the values of:

(a) xyz;   (b) $xy + z$;   (c) $x - yz$;   (d) $(x - y)z$.

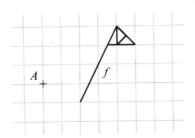

Figure 1

6   Copy Figure 1 onto squared paper and draw the image of the flag f under a rotation of $90°$ (anti-clockwise) about the point A.

REVISION EXERCISE 6

1   Write the following numbers in standard form:

(a) the number of seconds in one day;

(b) the number of hours in one year;

(c) the number of square millimetres in one hectare;

(d) the number of cents in six million dollars.

2   If $A = \{\text{factors of } 24\}$ and $B = \{\text{factors of } 42\}$ list $A \cup B$. What is $n(A \cap B)$?

3   Write the following in symbols.

(a) The cost of 5 kg of potatoes at x pence per kilogram and 2 kg of carrots at y pence per kilogram is less than £2.

(b) The area of a rectangle $4t$ metres long and $3t$ metres wide is at least $240\,\text{m}^2$.

4   Simplify:

(a) $3p - 2(2 - p)$;   (b) $4(2p - 3q) + 3(5q - 3p)$;

(c) $3(r + s) - 2(r - s)$;   (d) $\dfrac{15r^2 s}{3rs}$.

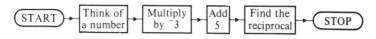

Figure 2

5 The function f is given by the flow chart in Figure 2.
  (a) Find $f(2), f(0)$ and $f(-\frac{1}{3})$.
  (b) Write f in the form $f : x \longrightarrow \ldots$
6 (a) Write down the values of x^2 and x^3 if
    (i) $x = 2$;   (ii) $x = \,^-2$;   (iii) $x = 0.2$;   (iv) $x = \,^-0.2$.
  (b) For what values of x is it true that:
    (i) $x = x^2 = x^3$;   (ii) $x^3 > x^2 > x$;   (iii) $x^2 > x > x^3$?

REVISION EXERCISE 7

1 Find (without using a calculator):
  (a) 0.05^2;   (b) $0.01 \div 0.1$;   (c) $0.7 \times 0.4 \times 0.25$;   (d) $\dfrac{4 \times 10^{-3}}{1.2 \times 10^{-3} - 2 \times 10^{-4}}$.

2 Simplify:
  (a) $2w - 3w + 5w$;   (b) $\dfrac{3x}{4} - \dfrac{x}{3}$;   (c) $\dfrac{2y^2}{5} \times \dfrac{10}{y}$;   (d) $2(2y - 3z) - 3(y - 2z)$.

3 If $\mathscr{E} = \{1, 2, 3, 4, 5, 6, 7, 8, 9, 10\}$, $A = \{n : 5 < n \leqslant 8\}$ and $B = \{n : 1 < n < 7\}$ draw a Venn diagram with the numbers 1 to 10 written in their appropriate regions. What is $n(A \cup B)$?

4 Find n if:
  (a) $0.0072 = 7.2 \times 10^n$;   (b) $80\,300 = 8.03 \times 10^n$;
  (c) $\sqrt{(1.6 \times 10^{11})} = 4 \times 10^n$;   (d) $10^n \times 10^{-4} = 10^{-9}$.

5 Calculate the area of the triangular region bounded by the lines $y = 2x$, $x + y = 6$ and the x-axis.

6 On squared paper, using a scale of 1 cm for 1 unit, plot the points $O(0, 0)$, $A(3, 4)$ and $B(6, 3)$. Making your methods clear,
  (a) construct $l = \{P : PA = PB\}$;
  (b) construct m, the bisectors of the angle between OA and the x-axis.
Write down the coordinates of the members of $l \cap m$.

8

Ratio and percentage

1. RATIOS

Like quantities can be compared by using ratios. For example, the statements 'this plant is twice as tall as that one', 'Concorde flies at twice the speed of sound', and 'this orange is twice as heavy as that apple' all use the idea of a ratio of 2:1 in comparing heights, speeds or weights.

Ratios can be multiplied or divided by any number (except zero) to obtain an equivalent ratio. For example:

$$2:3, \quad 4:6, \quad 20:30, \quad 5:7\tfrac{1}{2}, \quad \tfrac{2}{3}:1 \text{ and } 1:1.5 \text{ are all equivalent.}$$

When a ratio is written in the form $1:n$, n is called the *scale factor*. So the scale factor corresponding to all the ratios above is $1\tfrac{1}{2}$.

Ratios are sometimes used to describe the way in which a quantity is shared. If Alan, Brian and Catherine share £6 in the ratio 1:3:4 then there are 8 shares of which Alan has one, Brian three and Catherine four.

Alan has $\tfrac{1}{8}$ of £6 = £0.75;
Brian has $\tfrac{3}{8}$ of £6 = £2.25; and
Catherine has $\tfrac{4}{8}$ of £6 = £3.

Exercise A

*1   Write down in the form $1:n$ ratios which are equivalent to the following:
  (a) 3p:42p; (b) 12p:£1.80; (c) 4 days:4 weeks;
  (d) 0.3 m:12 m; (e) 0.4 kg:0.012 kg; (f) 0.27 km:270 m.

2   Write down in the form $m:1$ ratios which are equivalent to the following:
  (a) £15:5p; (b) 3p:40p; (c) 0.24 kg:0.8 g;
  (d) 1 day:1 second; (e) 0.44 kg:8 tonne; (f) 3.5×10^{11}m:5×10^7 m.

*3   The mass of the moon is 7.35×10^{22} kg, the mass of the earth is 5.97×10^{24} kg, and the mass of the sun is 1.99×10^{30} kg. Express the following ratios in the form $1:n$
  (a) mass of moon : mass of earth;
  (b) mass of earth : mass of sun;
  (c) mass of moon : mass of sun.

4   The diameter of the moon is 3.48×10^6 m, the diameter of the earth is 1.27×10^7 m, and the diameter of the sun is 1.39×10^9 m. Express the following ratios in the form $1:n$
  (a) diameter of moon : diameter of earth;
  (b) diameter of earth : diameter of sun;
  (c) diameter of moon : diameter of sun.

*5   (a) Share £5.40 in the ratio 5:4.
  (b) Share 98 kg in the ratio 4:2:1.
  (c) Share 140 km in the ratio 4:3:2:1.

6 A 400-metre running track is to be designed so that the ratio of the length of the straight sections to the length of the curved sections is 3 : 2. What is the length of each straight?

*7 (a) Share 360 in the ratio 2 : 3 : 4.

(b) In the recent Transylvanian election the votes cast were as follows:

Vampire Party	20 000
Werewolf Conservation Party	30 000
Bloodsuckers Coalition	40 000

Draw a pie chart to represent this information.

8 Draw a pie chart to illustrate the following data:

Strength of the Armed Forces, 1979

Royal Navy and Royal Marines	72 500
Army	156 200
Royal Air Force	86 300

*9 The ratio of the masses of hydrogen and oxygen in each molecule of water is 2.02 : 16. What mass of oxygen is there in 1 kg of water?

10 In 1972, 430 000 boys and 404 000 girls were born in Britain. Of a group of 1000 people born in 1972, how many would you expect to be girls?

2. PERCENTAGES

A percentage is a fraction in which the denominator is 100. For example,

$$8\% \text{ means } \frac{8}{100} \text{ or } 0.08 \,.$$

So 8% of £16 $= 0.08 \times £16 = £1.28$.

Fractions can be written as decimals or percentages. For example:

$$\frac{1}{2} = 0.5 = \frac{50}{100} = 50\%\,;$$

$$\frac{3}{25} = 0.12 = \frac{12}{100} = 12\%\,;$$

$$\frac{7}{40} = 0.175 = \frac{17\frac{1}{2}}{100} = 17\frac{1}{2}\%\,;$$

$$\frac{2}{3} = 0.6 \approx \frac{67}{100} = 67\%.$$

Exercise B

*1 Write the following fractions as percentages:

(a) $\frac{1}{4}$; (b) $\frac{1}{20}$; (c) $\frac{11}{25}$; (d) $\frac{2}{7}$.

2 Write the following fractions as percentages:

(a) $\frac{1}{3}$; (b) $\frac{3}{11}$; (c) $\frac{12}{5}$; (d) $\frac{5}{8}$.

*3 Write the following percentages as fractions in their simplest form:

(a) 20%; (b) 15%; (c) $12\frac{1}{2}\%$; (d) 125%.

4 Write the following percentages as fractions in their simplest form:

(a) 35%; (b) 88%; (c) 250%; (d) $133\frac{1}{3}\%$.

*5 Copy and complete these calculations:
   (a) 5% of £24 = 0.05 × £24 = ...
   (b) 35% of 3600 sheep = 0.35 × 3600 sheep = ...
   (c) 49% of 16 447 votes = ...
   (d) 112% of £60.50 = ...

6 Calculate the following:
   (a) 16% of £14.75;   (b) 15% of 480 km;
   (c) 8% of 88p;   (d) $107\frac{1}{2}$% of 0.48 kg.

*7 (a) What percentage of £60 is £5.40?
   (b) A guy-rope of original length 80 cm shrinks 1.2 cm when wet. Express this as a percentage of its original length.
   (c) 2749 votes were cast at a district election. 893 people voted for Councillor Solomon. What percentage of the votes did he receive?
   (d) Express 346 g as a percentage of 2.00 kg.

8 (a) 'Every kilogram of strawberry jam contains 360 g of strawberries.' What percentage is this?
   (b) The area of the earth's oceans is about 3.6×10^8 km^2. What percentage of the total surface area of the earth (5.1×10^8 km^2) is this?
   (c) The population of Great Britain in 1971 was 55.6 million. The population of Greater London in the same year was 7.45 million. What percentage of the population of Britain lived in Greater London?
   (d) The corresponding figures from the 1911 census were 42.1 million and 7.16 million. What was the corresponding percentage?

*9 Write down an expression for 6% of £x.

10 Write down an expression for r% of £x.

3. PERCENTAGE INCREASES

On 1 June 1979, Sump Cars announced a 7% increase in the price of their 15GTX. If the price before the increase was £4329.57, what was the new price?

Every £100 of the old price has been increased by 7% to £107, so the price has been multiplied by

$$\frac{107}{100} = 1.07.$$

The new price is therefore £4329.57 × 1.07 = £4632.64.

Every percentage increase can be interpreted as multiplying by a scale factor. For example, if a length is increased by 20%, the ratio of the original length to the new length is

$$100:120 \quad = \quad 1:\frac{120}{100} \quad = \quad 1:1.20,$$

so the length has been multiplied by 1.2.

Example 4

The population of Umbridge increased by 37% during the years 1960–80. If the population in 1960 was 447, what was the population in 1980?

An increase of 37% is equivalent to multiplying by 1.37, so the population in 1980 was $447 \times 1.37 = 612$.

Example 5

The height of a tree increased from 2.73 m to 2.98 m in one year. What percentage increase is this?

The height has been multiplied by a factor of $\dfrac{2.98}{2.73} \approx 1.09$.

It has increased by approximately 9%.

Example 6

The price of a picture, including value added tax at 15% is £27.60. What is the price exclusive of VAT?

VAT is added to the original price at a rate of 15% of the original price. So the ratio of the price exclusive of VAT to the price including VAT is 1 : 1.15.

Price exclusive of VAT ———— Multiply by 1.15 ———— Price including VAT

Price exclusive of VAT ———— Divide by 1.15 ———— Price including VAT

We must therefore *divide* the price including VAT by 1.15 to obtain:
Price exclusive of VAT $= £27.60 \div 1.15 = £24$.

Exercise C

In questions 1–4, use a single calculation in each case to find the new quantities when:
 *1 £16.25 is increased by 12%;
 2 a piece of elastic thread of length 79 cm is stretched by 11%;
 *3 the population (106 432) of the city of Westfield increases by 5%;
 4 the height of a sapling (2.4 m) increases by 125%.
In questions 5–8, find the price including VAT.
 *5 £39.60 plus 15% VAT;
 6 £24.20 plus 15% VAT;
 *7 DM 7.80 plus 13% Mehrwertsteuer (West German VAT);
 8 355 fr. plus 17.6% taxe à la valeur ajoutée (French VAT).
In questions 9–12, find the prices exclusive of VAT.
 *9 £7.89 including VAT at 15%;
 10 £57.83 including VAT at 15%;
 *11 145 fr. including taxe à la valeur ajoutée at 17.6%;
 12 DM 40.00 including Mehrwertsteuer at 13%.
 *13 The population of Villanova has increased by 63% during the last five years and is now 124 000. What was its population five years ago?
 14 The price of houses in Villanova has increased by 18% during the last year. If a house costs $45 000 now, what would it have cost a year ago?

*15   The leaf-area of a plant increased by 12% during a week. At the end of the week the leaf-area was 47 cm². What was it at the beginning of the week?

16   A clothes-line stretches by 3% of its original length. What length of line will be needed to give a stretched length of 6.2 m?

*17   The price of a cup of tea on Ruritanian Railways' trains was 31 ruples last year and is now 36 ruples. By what percentage has the price increased?

18   The mass of a tortoise increased from 2.47 kg to 2.78 kg during a year. What percentage increase is this?

*19   The table below shows the population of the United Kingdom at various censuses.

Year	1911	1931	1951	1971
Population (thousands)	42 082	46 038	50 225	55 615

Calculate the percentage increases in the population:
(a) between 1911 and 1931;
(b) between 1931 and 1951;
(c) between 1951 and 1971;
(d) between 1911 and 1971.

20   (a) In 1962 there were 779 000 11-year-olds in schools in Britain; in 1977 the number was 950 000. What percentage increase is this?
(b) The corresponding figures for 17-year-olds were 97 000 and 181 000. Calculate the percentage increase in this case.
Would you have expected your answers to (a) and (b) to be very different? Why?

4. MORE INCREASES

In May 1979, Sump Cars offered their 15GTX at a price of £4329.57. On 1 June 1979, an increase of 7% was announced, resulting in a price of £4329.57 × 1.07 = £4632.64 (see page 100).

On 1 December 1979, a further increase of 8% was announced. The December price therefore was £4632.64 × 1.08 = £5003.25. The May price has been multiplied in turn by 1.07 and by 1.08 so that the December price is

$$£4329.57 \times 1.07 \times 1.08 = £4329.57 \times 1.1556 = £5003.25.$$

The December price is therefore the May price × 1.1556, a total increase of 15.56%.

Notice that the two scale factors are multiplied together and *not* added. We can always find the effect of two successive percentage increases by multiplying the scale factors. For example, an increase of 12% followed by an increase of 25% is equivalent to multiplying by 1.12 × 1.25 = 1.4, which is an increase of 40%. Does the order of the increases matter?

Exercise D

In questions 1–8, find the total percentage increase in each case.
*1   An increase of 10% followed by an increase of 20%.
2   An increase of 8% followed by an increase of 22%.
*3   An increase of 5% followed by an increase of 25%.
4   Two successive increases of 15%.

*5 Two successive increases of 50%.

6 An increase of 20% followed by an increase of 30% and then 50%.

*7 Three successive increases of 33%.

8 Four successive increases of 25%

*9 The height of a sapling was 2.11m. In the next three years its height increased by 15%, 5% and 10%. What was its height at the end of those three years?

10 On Monday at 9 a.m. a population of bacteria was estimated at 3000. If the population increases by 10% every 24 hours, what will it be at 9 a.m. on the following Saturday?

5. PERCENTAGE DECREASES

When, in a sale, a dress is sold at '10% off' or at '10% discount', every 100p of the old price has been decreased by 10% to 90p, so the price has been multiplied by a scale factor of $\frac{90}{100} = 0.90$. We can use scale factors like these to solve problems involving percentage reductions.

Example 7

A 2-metre length of cloth shrinks by 10% and 5% in two successive washings. What is its new length?

The shrinkings involve scale factors of 0.90 and 0.95, so the new length is $2 \text{ m} \times 0.90 \times 0.95 = 1.71 \text{ m}$.

Example 8

The number of British Rail passenger carriages in use in 1968 was 19 528. In 1978 it was 16 601. What percentage decrease is this?

The number has decreased by a factor of $\dfrac{16\ 601}{19\ 528} \approx 0.85$.

The percentage decrease is approximately $100 - 85 = 15$.

Example 9

After a 15% reduction the price of a suit is £39.95. What was the original price?

A reduction of 15% is given by a scale factor of 0.85, so the original price must have been £39.95 ÷ 0.85 = £47.

Example 10

A colony of Chalkhill Blue butterflies is estimated to be decreasing in size by 20% per year over the period 1978–81. In summer 1980, it was estimated that there were about 600 butterflies in the colony.

(a) What is its size expected to be in 1981?

(b) What was the size of the colony in (i) 1979, (ii) 1978?

(c) If the same rate of decrease continues, when would the colony contain less than 300 butterflies?

If the population decreases by 20% each year, then for every 100 butterflies in 1980 there are only 80 in 1981. The size of the colony is reduced by a scale factor of 0.8 each year.

(a) In 1981, we expect the number of butterflies to be $600 \times 0.8 = 480$ (or, let us say, just under 500, since the figures are evidently rough estimates).

(b) (i) In 1979 the number of butterflies was about $\dfrac{600}{0.8} = 750$;

(ii) In 1978 the number of butterflies was about $\dfrac{600}{0.8^2}\left(\text{or}\dfrac{750}{0.8}\right) = 937.5$,

or, let us say, between 900 and 950.

(c) If we start with 600 and multiply by 0.8 again and again, we find that
$$600 \times 0.8^3 = 307.2$$
and $$600 \times 0.8^4 = 245.76$$

so the size of the colony will be about 300 in 1983 and would be less than 300 in 1984.

Exercise E

*1   Write down the scale factors corresponding to the following percentage decreases:
(a) 8%;   (b) 18%;   (c) 25%;   (d) 50%.

2   Write down the scale factors corresponding to the following percentage decreases:
(a) 36%;   (b) 72%;   (c) 99%;   (d) 100%.

In questions 3–6, use a single calculation in each case to find the new quantities when:

*3   the price of a dress, £23, is reduced by 15%;

4   a second-hand car, priced at £1500, is sold at $12\frac{1}{2}\%$ discount, for cash;

*5   a rope of length 31.30 m shrinks $1\frac{1}{2}\%$ when wet;

6   the population of medieval Umbrigge, 537 souls, is reduced by 37% by the plague.

*7   The number of kilometres of rail routes open for traffic in Britain fell from 20 031 in 1968 to 17 901 in 1978. What percentage decrease is this?

8   Cinema admissions in 1968 were 237 million; in 1978 they were 126 million. What percentage decrease is this?

*9   The consumption of tea in Britain fell from 73.4 g per person per week to 56.4 g per person per week between 1968 and 1978. What percentage decrease is this?

10   As a 'pre-publication offer' a book is priced at £12.95 instead of its publication price of £13.95. What percentage discount is this?

*11   The number of pupils at Sampsey High School is 6% less this year than it was last year. This year there are 530 pupils. How many were there last year?

12   After a 10% reduction the price of a camera is £40.95. What was its price before?

*13   Myxomatosis reduced the population of rabbits on the Isle of Sampsey by 95%. If there are now 2000 rabbits on the island, how many were there before the disease struck?

14   A shop sells CVM 2000R calculators at '20% below the manufacturer's recommended price' for £12.40.

(*a*) What was the manufacturer's recommended price?

(*b*) In the January sales the shop takes a further 10% off all prices. What does the CVM 2000R then cost?

*15   An antique dealer marks the sale price of a Louis XV commode chest at 50% above the £9500 he paid for it at auction.

(*a*) What is his sale price?

(*b*) By what percentage can he reduce the sale price without making a loss?

16   A radioactive element decays at a rate of 11.3% per hour.

(*a*) By what percentage is its mass reduced: (i) after 2 hours; (ii) after 5 hours?

(*b*) What is the half-life of the element, to the nearest hour? (The half-life is the time taken for half the mass to disintegrate.)

*17   A slimming diet is believed to result in a reduction of weight of 1% per day. How long will a 130 kg man need to diet to reduce his weight below 110 kg?

18   It is estimated that the area of forest in the state of Sylvania is decreasing at a rate of 10% a year. The area of forest in 1980 was 275 km².

(*a*) What was the area of forest: (i) in 1979;   (ii) in 1975?

(*b*) What is the area of forest expected to be (i) in 1981;   (ii) in 1990?

SUMMARY

Like quantities are compared by ratios. When a ratio is written in the form 1: n the number n is called the scale factor.   (Section 1)

A percentage is a fraction whose denominator is 100.   (Section 2)

Increasing a quantity by 9% is equivalent to multiplying it by a scale factor of 1.09.   (Section 3)

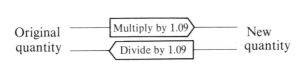

For a decrease of 9% the scale factor is 0.91.   (Section 5)

The effect of successive percentage changes can be found by multiplying together the corresponding scale factors.   (Section 4)

Summary exercise

1   Write down in the form 1 : n ratios equivalent to:

(*a*) height of the London Post Office Tower (189 m): height of the Eiffel Tower, Paris (322 m);

(*b*) velocity of sound in air (331 m/s): velocity of sound in water (1410 m/s).

2   The line segment AB is 15.4 cm long. Q is a point on AB and the ratio $AQ:QB$ is 4:1. What is the length of AQ?

3   Write the following as percentages:

(*a*) 0.15;   (*b*) $\frac{3}{5}$;   (*c*) $1\frac{1}{3}$;   (*d*) 2.34.

4   Calculate:
(a) 0.03% of £1500;   (b) 24% of 24 hours.

5   The height of a tree increases by 13% in a year. If its height at the beginning of the year is 6.5 m, what is its height at the end of the year?

6   A starving yak loses 13% of its mass in a month. If its mass at the beginning of the month is 390 kg, what is its mass at the end of the month?

7   The Dead Sea is slowly drying up. The maximum depth in 1900 was 421 m. In 1980 it was 411 m. What percentage decrease is this?

8   Find the single percentage increase or decrease equivalent to:
(a) an increase of 30% followed by an increase of 40%;
(b) a decrease of 30% followed by a decrease of 40%;
(c) an increase of 10% followed by a decrease of 10%;
(d) a decrease of 20% followed by an increase of 25%.

9   The price of a Silver Whisper car was increased by 14% to £45 600. What was its price before the increase?

10 The population of Blighton is decreasing at a rate of 6% a year. If its population in 1980 was 23 000,
(a) what was its population in 1979;
(b) what is its population expected to be in 1985?

Miscellaneous exercise

1   It takes 0.70 mg of ascorbic acid (vitamin C) to change the colour of the indicator known as DCPIP. If 1 ml of fresh lemon juice contains 3.5 mg of ascorbic acid, how much fresh lemon juice will be required to change the colour of DCPIP?

2   When potassium hydroxide solution is added to a sample of air, any carbon dioxide is quickly absorbed and the air decreases in volume. If potassium pyrogallate is then added to the same sample, any oxygen will also be absorbed and the air will decrease further in volume.
    In such an experiment, an air sample of volume 22.0 cm^3 is used. After adding potassium hydroxide the volume reduces to 21.1 cm^3. After adding potassium pyrogallate the volume further reduces to 16.9 cm^3.
(a) Find the volume of carbon dioxide and the volume of oxygen present in the original sample.
(b) Express the volume of each of these gases as a percentage of the original volume of the sample.

3   A specimen of muscle fibre was cut from a piece of fresh lean meat and measured 23 mm. Drops of ATP, applied with a hypodermic syringe, caused the specimen to contract to a length of 14 mm. Express the new length as a percentage of the original length.
    A second specimen, of original length 29 mm, contracted under the same treatment to 18 mm. Which of the two specimens showed the greater percentage contraction?

4   Fable Books Ltd £1 ordinary shares cost £1.53 on the stock market. Their 12% dividend yields an income to shareholders of 12% × £1 per share. If £350 is invested in the shares,
(a) how many whole shares are bought;
(b) what income is received from the dividend?

5 The various uses of coal in England over a period of one year are shown in the following table:

Domestic	14×10^6 tonne
Power stations	72×10^6 tonne
Industry	19×10^6 tonne
Coke ovens	20×10^6 tonne

Show this information in a pie chart, writing in each sector of the chart the corresponding percentage of total coal consumption.

6 Find the new weights when:

   (a) a caterpillar, weighing 23.5 g, eats enough nettle leaves to increase its weight by 12.5%;

   (b) a caterpillar, weighing 31.2 g, sheds its skin, thus decreasing its weight by 2.1%.

7 Weed on the surface of a reservoir covered an area of 262 m^2 on 1 January 1978 and had spread to cover an area of 631 m^2 one year later.

   (a) (i) By what scale factor had the area covered increased in one year?

       (ii) What percentage increase is this?

   (b) Assuming the same percentage increase each year, what area would be covered by weed by 1 January 1984?

   (c) If chemical spraying, estimated to halve the scale factor, is applied from 1 January 1980, what area would be covered by weed by 1 January 1984?

8 A compound weighed 2.66 g after 20 minutes heating. If it weighed 3.09 g initially, and the loss of weight was caused by loss of water of crystallisation to the atmosphere, calculate the percentage of water of crystallisation present initially.

9 A car, priced at £4500 new, is likely to lose 25% of its value in the first year. Depreciation (loss of value) then continues at about 20% per year for the next 5 years. What is it worth:

   (a) after 1 year;   (b) after 2 years;   (c) after 6 years?

10 A force is applied to a length of wire and stretches it by 23%. When the force is removed the length decreases by 9% to 0.83 m. What was its original length?

9

Accuracy

1. NUMBERS USED IN MEASUREMENT

Making measurements

When you measure something, the accuracy of your measurement depends on various things:
(1) the accuracy and suitability of the measuring instrument;
(2) the nature of the quantity being measured;
(3) the accuracy with which it is humanly possible to read the measuring instrument.

Which of these factors are most significant when you (and some friends, perhaps) measure (a) the time taken for someone to walk the length of the classroom; (b) the time taken for an object to reach the ground when dropped?

Which of these factors are most significant (a) when measuring an electric current with an ammeter; (b) when measuring a temperature with a thermometer?

If you are measuring the length of a field, it may be hard to decide exactly where the field begins and ends, there may be bumps in the middle of it, or a strong wind blowing so that a measuring tape will not lie flat and straight; measuring tapes are inclined to stretch; the field may be longer than the tape (what do you do about this? – might this involve more error?). To how many significant figures is it reasonable to give the result if the field is about 200 m long?

If you are measuring the inside of a cupboard in order to fit a shelf it may be hard to get your eye anywhere near the scale on the tape or rule in order to read it; if the line of view from your eye to the scale is not perpendicular to the scale, the reading will be inaccurate (this is known as 'parallax' error). What other difficulties may there be in making a measurement of this sort? To how many significant figures is it reasonable to give the dimensions of the shelf needed if the cupboard is about 90 cm wide and 30 cm deep?

What difficulties are encountered in measuring someone's height? How accurately can a person's height reasonably be given?

Use a ruler to measure the lengths of the sides of this book. How accurately can you measure these lengths? Will you obtain the same answers with another ruler? Will someone else (as careful as you!) obtain the same answers? If you are very careful and use a good-quality ruler, can such lengths be measured reliably to the nearest millimetre?

Specifying measurements

In measuring the dimensions of a small rigid object, such as a machine part being turned on a lathe, vernier callipers or a micrometer screw gauge may be used. If the diameter of a metal rod is given as 0.362 cm it means that as far as can be judged from the scale, the diameter is nearer to 0.362 cm than to 0.361 cm or 0.363 cm, i.e. that

$$0.3615 \text{ cm} \leqslant \text{diameter} < 0.3625 \text{ cm.}$$

(If it is impossible to decide between two readings, there are a number of possible actions. One possibility is always to give the higher number; another is to give the higher or lower in such a way that the last digit is even. We have assumed that the former course of action has been taken.)

When someone manufacturing a part for a machine reads his drawing, he may find a width given in a different form:
0.520 ± 0.001 cm, say. This means:

$$0.519 \text{ cm} \leqslant \text{length} \leqslant 0.521 \text{ cm}$$

and shows how much room for error he can allow himself. The ± 0.001 cm is known as the 'tolerance'.

Here are some further examples of these inequalities:
(1) Current = 1.5 A means
$$1.45 \text{ A} \leqslant \text{current} < 1.55 \text{A.}$$
(2) Temperature = 273.0 K means
$$272.95 \text{ K} \leqslant \text{temperature} < 273.05 \text{ K.}$$
But temperature = 273 K means
$$272.5 \text{ K} \leqslant \text{temperature} < 273.5 \text{ K.}$$
(3) Diameter = 0.825 ± 0.002 cm means
$$0.823 \text{ cm} \leqslant \text{diameter} \leqslant 0.827 \text{ cm.}$$
(4) Resistivity = 2.5×10^{-6} Ω m means
$$2.45 \times 10^{-6} \text{ Ω m} \leqslant \text{resistivity} < 2.55 \times 10^{-6} \text{Ω m.}$$
(5) Length = 250 m to 2 s.f. means
$$245 \text{m} \leqslant \text{length} < 255 \text{m.}$$

Exercise A

1 How accurately can you weigh using a chemical balance?

2 How accurately can you read the volume of liquid in a bottle? It is important to position your eye so that you are looking in a direction perpendicular to the column of liquid, and then to read at the level of the bottom of the meniscus (or the top in the case of mercury – why?).

*3 Write each of the following measurements in the form of the equivalent inequality:
    (a) length = 13.7 m;   (b) length = 13.07 m;
    (c) length = 13.70 m;   (d) time = 31.9 s.

4 Write each of the following measurements in the form of the equivalent inequality:
    (a) volume = 12 l;   (b) volume = 2.0 l;
    (c) area = 0.0801 m^2;   (d) area = 0.00800 m^2.

*5 Write each of the following measurements in the form of the equivalent inequality:

(*a*) speed = 3000 m/s to an accuracy of four significant figures;

(*b*) speed = 3000 m/s to an accuracy of one significant figure;

(*c*) temperature = 80°C to an accuracy of two significant figures;

(*d*) area = 50 000m² to an accuracy of three significant figures.

6 Write each of the following measurements in the form of the equivalent inequality:

(*a*) length = 3×10^4 m;   (*b*) length = 3.0×10^4 m;

(*c*) area = 3.00×10^4 m²;   (*d*) area = 3.0000×10^6 m².

7 The following readings were all taken from the same measuring instrument in the same experiment.

Current in amperes: 0.85,   0.87,   0.9,   0.92,   0.96,   1,   1.02

(*a*) What does the reading 0.85 A mean, as an inequality?

(*b*) How should the reading given as 0.9 A really have been given?

(*c*) Which other reading has been written down inadequately? How should it have been given?

2. COMBINING MEASUREMENTS

Measurements often have to be combined in some way: for example, an average speed may be calculated by dividing a distance measurement by a time measurement, or the perimeter of a field may be calculated by adding together several different measurements of lengths along its boundaries. The final results of such calculations can never be known to greater accuracy than the least accurate of the measurements involved.

If the length, L cm, of a piece of paper is recorded as 12.6 cm it means that $12.55 \leqslant L < 12.65$. If the width, W cm, is recorded as 9.0 cm it means that $8.95 \leqslant W < 9.05$. If the area ($L \times W$ cm²) is now calculated as 12.6×9.0 the result is 113.4. Is it then correct to give the area as 113.4 cm²?

In fact the area, A cm², cannot be known for certain to this accuracy. What is certain is that the area cannot be smaller than 8.95×12.55 cm² and that it must be less than 9.05×12.65 cm².

i.e. $8.95 \times 12.55 \leqslant A < 9.05 \times 12.65$

$112.3225 \leqslant A < 114.4825$

112.3225 is known as the 'lower bound' for the value of A;

114.4825 is known as the 'upper bound' for the value of A.

It would therefore be misleading to give the area as 113.4 cm² since that would suggest that $113.35 \leqslant A < 113.45$, and we cannot be sure of this.

We could, however, use the bounds to write the area as 113.4 ± 1.1 cm².

In practical problems involving calculations from measurements it would be a nuisance to have to calculate the upper and lower bounds every time. We shall adopt a convention that an answer will be given to the same number of significant figures as the least accurate of the original measurements. But we shall need to examine from time to time whether this convention is reasonable for a particular calculation. The only sure way of knowing the accuracy of an answer is to calculate the upper and lower bounds.

In the above example the measurement of the width was given as 9.0 cm, to 2 s.f. The area, calculated as 113.4 cm^2, would therefore be given as '110 cm^2 to two significant figures'. We are claiming that

$$105 \leqslant A < 115$$

and this is certainly true.

Presenting the results of calculations

In order that you, or someone else reading your working, can check the working easily, it is important to set out clearly the results of calculations. When you are using a calculator to help you, you should write down the whole of the result displayed and then, if necessary, correct it to an appropriate number of significant figures. It can also be helpful to indicate by some suitable short-hand when a calculator has been used. We shall use $\boxed{\text{c}}$.

Example 1
    Find the area of the L-shaped field shown in Figure 1.

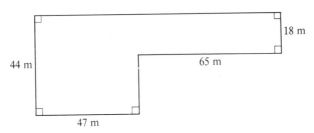

Figure 1

Area of field $= (44 \times 47 + 65 \times 18) \text{ m}^2$
$\qquad\qquad = (2068 + 1170) \text{ m}^2 \qquad \boxed{\text{c}}$
$\qquad\qquad = 3238 \text{ m}^2$
$\qquad\qquad \approx 3200 \text{ m}^2$ (to 2 s.f.)
Notice that the complete calculator display should be retained for intermediate stages of the calculation. For example, if we had corrected answers to an accuracy of two significant figures as we proceeded in the calculation above, we would have obtained
    Area $= (44 \times 47 + 65 \times 18) \text{ m}^2$
$\qquad \approx (2100 + 1200) \text{ m}^2 \qquad \boxed{\text{c}}$ (to 2 s.f.)
$\qquad = 3300 \text{ m}^2$ (to 2 s.f.)
which is incorrect.

Example 2
    Calculate the upper and lower bounds for the area of the field in Figure 1.

Upper bound $= (44.5 \times 47.5 + 65.5 \times 18.5) \text{ m}^2$
$\qquad\qquad\quad = (2113.75 + 1211.75) \text{ m}^2 \qquad \boxed{\text{c}}$
$\qquad\qquad\quad = 3325.5 \text{ m}^2$

Lower bound $= (43.5 \times 46.5 + 64.5 \times 17.5) \, \text{m}^2$
$= (2022.75 + 1128.75) \, \text{m}^2$ $\boxed{\text{C}}$
$= 3151.5 \, \text{m}^2$

Notice that the area could be written as (approximately) $3240 \pm 90 \, \text{m}^2$ so that our original answer of $3200 \, \text{m}^2$ to 2 s.f. is really too accurate.

Exercise B

*1   A rectangle has sides measured as 1.4 m and 2.5 m.
    (*a*) Calculate its area to 2 s.f. using these measurements.
    (*b*) Calculate the upper and lower bounds for the area. Is two significant figure accuracy reasonable in (*a*)?
    (*c*) Would it be correct to give the area as $3.5 \pm 0.1 \, \text{m}^2$? If not, give a correct version.

2   Repeat question 1 for a rectangle 6.8 m by 19.6 m.

*3   'Bildit' children's bricks have dimensions 2.0 cm by 2.0 cm by 4.0 cm. How many bricks could you be sure of fitting into a box whose internal measurements are 40.0 cm by 40.0 cm by 60.0 cm if:
    (*a*) the long sides of the bricks are placed parallel to the long side of the box;
    (*b*) the long sides of the bricks are placed parallel to one of the shorter sides of the box?

4   A packing-case 84 cm wide is to pass through a doorway 88 cm wide.
    (*a*) What is the total clearance on the two sides of the packing-case?
    (*b*) What are the upper and lower bounds for this clearance? Might a rope of thickness 1.4 cm which is tied round the packing-case have to be removed to get the case through the doorway?

Figure 2

*5   A cuboid is 7.5 m long, 8.5 m wide and 9.6 m high.
    (*a*) Calculate its volume from these measurements.
    (*b*) Calculate the upper and lower bounds for the volume.
    (*c*) To how many figures is your answer to (*a*) accurate?
    (*d*) Give the volume in the form $V \pm e \, \text{m}^3$.

6   Repeat question 5 for a cuboid 20.8 cm by 12.5 cm by 9.6 cm.

*7   A runner covers 100 m in 11.3 s.
    (*a*) Calculate his average speed from these measurements.
    (*b*) The upper bound for his speed is calculated from the upper bound for the

distance and the lower bound for the time. If the distance is accurate to the nearest metre, calculate the upper bound for his speed.

(c) If the distance is 100.0 m and the time 11.30 s, calculate the new upper bound for the runner's speed.

8 A car is timed between two marker-posts on a motorway. The distance between the posts is measured to be 297 m, and the car passes the second post 9.7 s after it passes the first one.

(a) Calculate the speed of the car using these measurements.

(b) Find the lower bound for the speed. Was the car breaking a 110 km/h speed limit?

*9 Calculate the following to an appropriate degree of accuracy.

(a) The time taken, in minutes, to walk 17.7 km at a steady speed of 4.8 km/h.

(b) The time taken, in minutes, to run 2.3 km at a speed of 9.9 km/h.

(c) The total time taken for (a) and (b).

10 Calculate the following to an appropriate degree of accuracy.

(a) The volume of 12 alloy ingots of dimensions 3.2 cm by 4.3 cm by 5.9 cm.

(b) The volume of 8 alloy ingots of dimensions 2.8 cm by 3.7 cm by 1.1 cm.

(c) The total volume of the 20 ingots described in (a) and (b).

(d) The total mass of the 20 ingots if the density of the alloy is 7.45×10^3 kg/m^3.

(e) The mass of copper in the ingots if 11.3% of the alloy (by mass) is copper.

SUMMARY

Physical measurements are not exact. For example:
$$\text{Length} = 4.6 \text{ m means} \quad 4.55 \text{ m} \leqslant \text{length} < 4.65 \text{ m}$$

$$\text{Time} = 2.3 \pm 0.2 \text{ s means} \quad 2.1 \text{ s} \leqslant \text{time} \leqslant 2.5 \text{ s} \qquad \text{(Section 1)}$$

Answers to calculations involving measurements should usually be given to the same number of significant figures as the least accurate of the original measurements. Such an answer may be more, or less, accurate than is justified; the only certain method is to calculate the upper and lower bounds.

Answers to calculations should be corrected to the appropriate number of significant figures at the last step. Accuracy may be needlessly lost if you do not retain all the figures until the end of the final calculation. (Section 2)

Summary exercise

1 Write each of the following in the form of an equivalent inequality:

(a) Length = 466 cm; (b) Volume = 2 cm^3;

(c) Mass = 8.001 kg; (d) Current = 2.99×10^{-3} A.

2 A man paces out a rectangular plot of land and estimates its length to be 170 m and its width to be 140 m, to the nearest 10 m. Calculate the upper and lower bounds for the area, using this information.

Using a measuring-tape, he finds that its length is 172 m and its width 139 m. Calculate the new upper and lower bounds.

3 Calculate the volume of the solid shown in Figure 3 to an appropriate degree of accuracy.

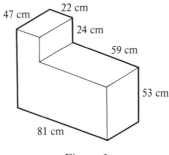

Figure 3

Miscellaneous exercise

1 An almost cubical block of metal measures 2.01 cm by 2.02 cm by 1.99 cm and its mass is found to be 52.34×10^{-3} kg. Calculate the density of the metal, in kilograms per cubic metre, by dividing its mass in kilograms by its volume in cubic metres. Give your answer to an appropriate degree of accuracy.

2 Calculate the velocity of sound, in metres per second, by multiplying the frequency of vibration of a tuning fork, 512 Hz, by the wavelength, 0.65 m, measured experimentally.

3 The effective resistance R, of two electrical resistors, having resistance R_1 and R_2, arranged in parallel, is given by the formula

$$R = \frac{1}{\dfrac{1}{R_1} + \dfrac{1}{R_2}}$$

Calculate the value of R if R_1 and R_2 are measured as $10.6\,\Omega$ and $15.2\,\Omega$ respectively, and give the answer accurate to a suitable number of significant figures. Then calculate the upper and lower bounds for R.

4 The time in seconds for the pendulum of a grandfather clock to swing in both directions is:

$$6.283 \sqrt{\left(\frac{l}{g}\right)},$$

where $g = 9.81$ and l m is the distance between the point of support and a mark on an adjustable weight attached to the pendulum. Find the value of l which makes the time 2.00 s.

5 The relative density of a substance is defined as the ratio:

$$\frac{\text{Mass of a certain volume of the substance}}{\text{Mass of the same volume of water}}$$

In an experiment to determine the density of lead, the following measurements were taken, using a 'density bottle':

Mass of density bottle empty	22.39 g
Mass of density bottle with some lead shot in it	81.02 g
Mass of density bottle with the lead shot in and then topped up with water	99.18 g
Mass of the density bottle with the lead emptied out and the bottle refilled to the top with water only	45.96 g

(a) Calculate the mass of lead in the bottle.

(b) Calculate the mass of water in the bottle when the bottle contained lead and water.

(c) Calculate the mass of water in the bottle when it contained water only.

(d) Calculate the mass of that volume of water which exactly replaced the lead, using answers (b) and (c).

(e) Calculate the relative density of lead from answers (a) and (d).

6    $$\text{Density (kg/m}^3) = \frac{\text{Mass (kg)}}{\text{Volume (m}^3)}$$

(a) Calculate the density of aluminium in kilograms per cubic metre if a cube of aluminium, the length of each side of which is 1.50 cm, has a mass 9.11 g.

(b) Estimate the mass of air in your classroom assuming that the density of air at the present temperature and pressure is about 1.3 kg/m^3.

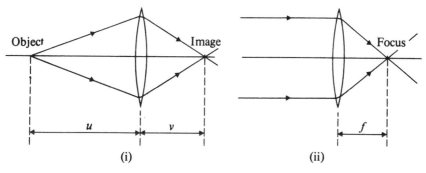

Figure 4

7 Figure 4 shows

(i) rays from a light source (object) at distance u from a convex lens, passing through the lens to form a real image at distance v from the lens;

(ii) parallel rays from the sun being brought to a focus at distance f from the lens.

The focal length of the lens, f, may be found using the formula

$$\frac{1}{f} = \frac{1}{u} + \frac{1}{v}$$

The power of the lens, F, in dioptres (D), may be found using the formula $F = \frac{1}{f}$, where f is measured in metres.

(a) Calculate the power of a lens having focal length 20.0 cm.

(b) In an experiment with a lens, the distances u cm and v cm are measured and it is found that $v = 13.5$ when $u = 18.6$. Calculate the power and focal length of this lens.

(c) An object is placed 50.0 cm from a 2.50-dioptre lens as in Figure 4. Calculate the image distance v cm.

8 The refractive index of water can be calculated as the ratio:

$$\frac{\text{Real depth of an object in the water}}{\text{Apparent depth of the object when viewed from vertically above}}$$

(a) Calculate the refractive index of water in a beaker if the real depth of an object on the bottom is 7.7 cm but the apparent depth was 5.8 cm. (Find out how the apparent depth can be measured if you do not know.)

(b) If a coin lies on the bottom of a swimming pool, 2.73 m below the surface, calculate the apparent depth of the coin below the surface as viewed from a diving board directly above.

(c) An experienced helicopter pilot sees a wreck below the surface of the sea. The wreck appears to him to be at a depth of about 8 m. Approximately how deep will the wreck really be?

10

Transformations

1. INTRODUCTION

This chapter is concerned with reflections, translations, rotations and enlargements and their properties. Figure 1 illustrates these four transformations and reminds you what information must be given to describe each one accurately.

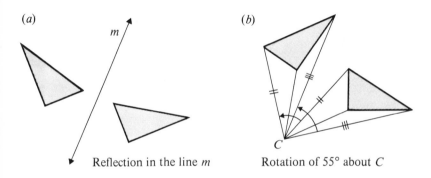

(a) Reflection in the line m

(b) Rotation of 55° about C

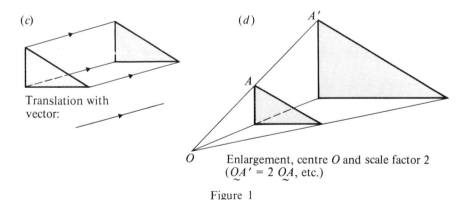

(c) Translation with vector:

(d) Enlargement, centre O and scale factor 2 ($\underset{\sim}{OA'} = 2\, \underset{\sim}{OA}$, etc.)

Figure 1

Figure 2 reminds you how to find the centre of a rotation. A has been rotated to A', so the centre of rotation, O, must be the same distance from A and A' and therefore lie on the mediator of AA'. Similarly it must lie on the mediator of BB', so it is at the point of intersection of these two mediators.

117

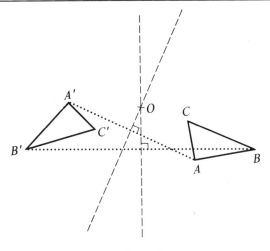

Figure 2

Exercise A

1   Copy Figure 3 on squared paper using the same scale. (Place *O* in the middle of the page.) Draw the images of the 'tick' *ABC* under
     (*a*) reflection in the line *m*;
     (*b*) reflection in the line *n*;
     (*c*) the rotation of ⁻90° (i.e. 90° clockwise) about *C*;
     (*d*) the rotation of 180° about *B*;
     (*e*) the translation with vector $C̰A$.
   Even if you have not needed tracing-paper to produce the images, use it now to provide a check.

2   Are all the images in question 1 the same shape and size? Which of the images are right-handed ticks and which are left-handed?

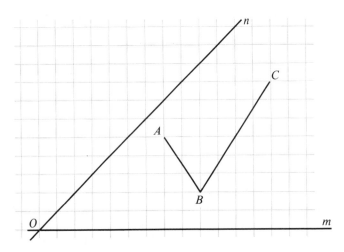

Figure 3

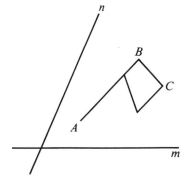

Figure 4

3 Copy Figure 4 approximately and then repeat question 1 for this flag as accurately as you can, using tracing-paper.

4 Copy Figure 5, placing *P* about 8 cm from the right-hand margin of your page and allowing about 5 cm of space above and below *P*. Draw the image of the flag under enlargement, centre *P* and scale factor 3. What are the lengths of the two flagpoles?

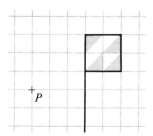

Figure 5

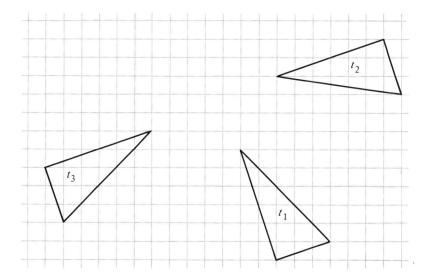

Figure 6

5 Copy Figure 6 and find:
  (*a*) the mirror line in which t_2 is the reflection of t_1;
  (*b*) the centre of the quarter-turn which maps t_3 onto t_1.

2. DIRECT AND OPPOSITE ISOMETRIES

Figure 7 shows the pattern of the blue parts of an inaccurately drawn Union Jack. If you cut a potato in half and carve it with a penknife, it is easy to produce a block that will enable you to print triangles with the aid of an ink pad. (See Figure 8).

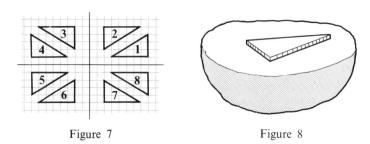

Figure 7   Figure 8

Will you be able to print all the triangles in Figure 7 with the block shown in Figure 8? If not, which of the numbered triangles would it print, and how many more potato blocks would be required? Describe them.

Consider very simple movements of the block from one position to another and try to describe these movements in terms of the transformations (*a*) rotation, (*b*) reflection or (*c*) translation. Can the block be moved in a way that corresponds to each of these transformations? If not, which is impossible?

If the potato printing were to be automated you would have to give the machine exact instructions. Having printed triangle 1, it would need to be told what movement to make before printing 2, 3 or whichever triangle you wanted it to print next. Discuss what instructions would be required for $\Delta 1 \longrightarrow \Delta 2$; $\Delta 2 \longrightarrow \Delta 5$; $\Delta 5 \longrightarrow \Delta 6$; what will have to happen before the remaining triangles can be printed? Discuss a suitable sequence for them.

You will have discovered that only rotation, reflection and translation are needed to move a triangle from one position to another. These three transformations are all *isometries* (Greek: *isos*, equal; *metron*, measure). Discuss the meaning of this word.

The block in Figure 8 would print triangle 1 but not triangle 3 because, although these two triangles are *congruent* (they have the same shape and size),

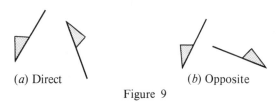

(*a*) Direct   (*b*) Opposite
Figure 9

one is 'back-to-front' compared with the other. We say that the triangles 1 and 3 are *oppositely* congruent.

In Figure 9 (*a*) the flags are *directly* congruent; in Figure 9 (*b*) they are oppositely congruent.

Translation and rotation will map a figure onto a directly congruent figure, so they are called *direct isometries*. Reflection maps a figure onto an oppositely congruent figure, so it is called an *opposite isometry*.

Exercise B

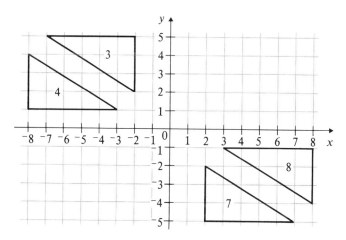

Figure 10

Questions 1–6 refer to Figure 10.

*1 What single transformation will map:
   (*a*) Δ3 onto Δ7;   (*b*) Δ3 onto Δ8 ?

2 Δ3 is given the translation with vector $\begin{bmatrix} 10 \\ 0 \end{bmatrix}$. Specify the second transformation which will map it:
   (*a*) onto Δ7;   (*b*) onto Δ8.

*3 Δ4 is reflected in the *y*-axis. State with reasons whether its image can be translated onto:
   (*a*) Δ8;   (*b*) Δ7.

4 Specify a pair of translations which will map Δ7 onto Δ4. Try to find two further pairs. How many such pairs are there? Do you need the diagram to help you specify them?

*5 Δ8 can be mapped onto Δ3 by means of a pair of rotations. If the first one maps Δ8 onto Δ7, specify each rotation. Will the same rotations performed in the reverse order have the same effect?

6 What translation must be given to Δ4 so that its image coincides with the image of Δ7 under the translation with vector $\begin{bmatrix} 2 \\ 6 \end{bmatrix}$?
Use your answer to find a pair of translations under which Δ7 ⟶ Δ4.

Questions 7–11 refer to Figure 11.

*7 If we start with the translation with vector $\begin{bmatrix} -6 \\ 1 \end{bmatrix}$, is there a rotation which will then map the image of Δ1 onto Δ2? If so, specify it. Discuss whether the same pair of transformations will work if applied in the opposite order (i.e. are they commutative?).

8 What single transformation, if any, will map:

    (a) Δ2 onto Δ7;   (b) Δ2 onto Δ1;
    (c) Δ2 onto Δ8?

*9 Δ2 is rotated through ⁻90° about the origin. Specify the second transformation needed to map its image onto Δ7.

10 Δ8 is rotated through 180° about (6, 1). Specify, if possible, a second transformation which will map its image:

    (a) onto Δ7;   (b) onto Δ2.

11 Δ2 is reflected in its longest side. Discuss which further triangles its image can now be mapped onto by a single rotation and why.

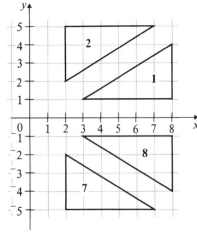

Figure 11

12 Is it *ever* possible for:

    (a) a rotation followed by a reflection to be equivalent to a translation;
    (b) a translation followed by a rotation to be equivalent to a reflection;
    (c) a reflection followed by another reflection to be equivalent to a rotation?

3. THE ALGEBRA OF TRANSFORMATIONS

It is useful to have a shorthand notation for transformations. We shall use capital letters, printed in bold type. So, for example, in this section we shall use **P** for the rotation of 90° about (1, 2) and **T** for the translation with vector $\begin{bmatrix} 4 \\ 0 \end{bmatrix}$. In writing we use $\underset{\sim}{P}$ and $\underset{\sim}{T}$ so that the transformations are clearly distinguished from points.

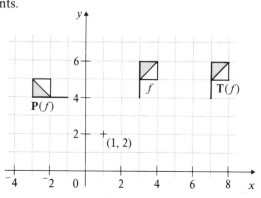

Figure 12

A flag f is shown in Figure 12. We write $\mathbf{P}(f)$ for its image under the rotation $\mathbf{P}$ and $\mathbf{T}(f)$ for its image under the translation $\mathbf{T}$. $\mathbf{P}(f)$ and $\mathbf{T}(f)$ are also shown in Figure 12.

If we now apply the rotation $\mathbf{P}$ to the flag $\mathbf{T}(f)$ we obtain $\mathbf{PT}(f)$, an abbreviation for $\mathbf{P}(\mathbf{T}(f))$. This may be read as 'P of T of f'. f, $\mathbf{T}(f)$ and $\mathbf{PT}(f)$ are shown in Figure 13.

Figure 14 shows f, $\mathbf{P}(f)$ and $\mathbf{TP}(f)$. Notice that $\mathbf{TP}(f)$ and $\mathbf{PT}(f)$ are different; the order in which the transformations have been carried out is different. To find $\mathbf{TP}(f)$ we do $\mathbf{P}$ first and then find the image of $\mathbf{P}(f)$ under the transformation $\mathbf{T}$.

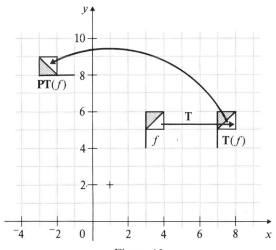

Figure 13

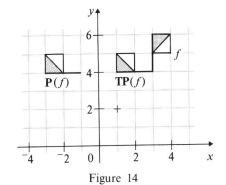

Figure 14

From Figure 14 we can see that f can be mapped onto $\mathbf{TP}(f)$ by the rotation of $90°$ about the point $(3, 4)$. We shall call this rotation $\mathbf{Q}$. Figure 15 shows another flag g together with $\mathbf{P}(g)$ and $\mathbf{TP}(g)$. Again g can be mapped onto $\mathbf{TP}(g)$ by the transformation $\mathbf{Q}$. When we are clear that $\mathbf{P}$ followed by $\mathbf{T}$ has the same effect as $\mathbf{Q}$ on any figure we care to draw, we can write

$$\mathbf{Q} = \mathbf{TP}.$$

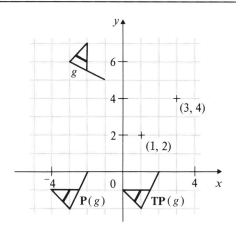

Figure 15

Exercise C

Questions 1–5 refer to Figure 16 and the following transformations:
    A: the rotation of 180° about (5, 3);
    B: the rotation of 180° about (5, ⁻3);
    C: the translation with vector $\begin{bmatrix} 10 \\ 6 \end{bmatrix}$;
    X: reflection in the x-axis;
    Y: reflection in the y-axis.
You may find tracing-paper useful to help you find the answers.

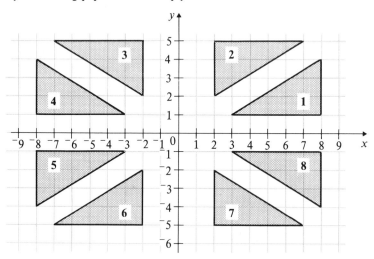

Figure 16

*1   State whether each of the following statements is true or false. Give a correct version of those which are false.
    (a) **A**(Δ1) = Δ2;   (b) **A**(Δ2) = Δ1;   (c) **C**(Δ5) = Δ1;   (d) **Y**(Δ4) = **X**(Δ8).

2   State whether each of the following statements is true or false. Give a correct version of those which are false.

(a) $\mathbf{AC}(\Delta 5) = \Delta 8$;   (b) $\mathbf{BC}(\Delta 6) = \Delta 2$;   (c) $\mathbf{XB}(\Delta 7) = \Delta 1$;
(d) $\mathbf{AC}(\Delta 6) = \mathbf{Y}(\Delta 4)$.

*3   Copy and complete the following:
   (a) $\mathbf{X}(\Delta 4) = \Delta$;   (b) $\mathbf{XB}(\Delta 7) = \mathbf{C}(\Delta$);   (c) $\mathbf{YB}(\Delta$ $) = \Delta 5$;
   (d) $(\Delta 2) = \Delta 8$.

4   (a) What does $\mathbf{CC}$ mean?
   (b) What are the coordinates of the image of the point ($^-8, ^-1$) under the transformation $\mathbf{CC}$?
   (c) What are the coordinates of the image of the point $(3, 1)$ under the transformation $\mathbf{CCC}$?
   (d) Suggest a shorter notation for $\mathbf{CC}$ and $\mathbf{CCC}$.

*5   State whether each of the following statements is true or false. Give a correct version of those which are false.
   (a) $\mathbf{AA}(\Delta 2) = \Delta 8$;   (b) $\mathbf{XX}(\Delta 4) = \mathbf{Y}(\Delta 1)$;   (c) $\mathbf{CC}(\Delta 6) = \mathbf{C}(\Delta 1)$;
   (d) $\mathbf{XX} = \mathbf{YY}$.

6   Take a sheet of paper and fold it in half, then fold it in half again. In the folded state cut out various shapes as in Figure 17. Draw freehand the pattern you expect to get when the paper is unfolded and then check that you are right.
   (a) What transformation maps the pattern in panel 2 (top left) onto the pattern in panel 3 (bottom left)?
   (b) What transformation maps the pattern in panel 1 onto the pattern in panel 3?
   (c) What is the name of the shape of the centre hole of the complete pattern? What symmetries does it have?

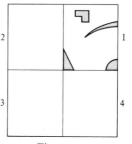

Figure 17

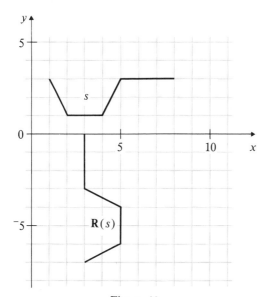

Figure 18

7   When answering this question allow space on your diagram for values of x between
    $^-5$ and 15 and values of y between $^-12$ and 12.

    Let **P** be the translation with vector $\begin{bmatrix} 6 \\ 8 \end{bmatrix}$,

    Q be the rotation of 90° about (0, 0)
    and **R** be the rotation of 90° about (7, $^-1$).
    Copy the 'saucepan' s in Figure 18. On the same diagram show **P**(s), **Q**(s), **R**(s),
    QR(s), **RQ**(s) and **RP**(s), labelling your images clearly.

*8 Describe fully the single transformations which in question 7 will:
    (a) map s onto **QR**(s);   (b) map s onto **RQ**(s);
    (c) map **R**(s) onto **RP**(s);   (d) map **RP**(s) onto **Q**(s).

9   Find the centres of the rotations which in question 7 will:
    (a) map s onto **RP**(s);   (b) map **R**(s) onto **P**(s).

10 When answering this question allow space on your diagram for values of x between
    $^-10$ and 15, and values of y between $^-5$ and 15.
    (a) Copy Figure 19, in which ABC has been given the enlargement **E** with scale
        factor 3 and centre the origin.
    (b) If **F** is enlargement with scale factor 3 and centre (8, 1), draw **F**($\triangle ABC$) and
        describe the single transformation which maps **F**($\triangle ABC$) onto **E**($\triangle ABC$).
    (c) If **G** is enlargement with scale factor $\frac{1}{2}$ and centre (6, $^-4$), draw **GE** ($\triangle ABC$)
        and find the centre of the single enlargement which maps $\triangle ABC$ onto
        GE($\triangle ABC$). What is the scale factor?

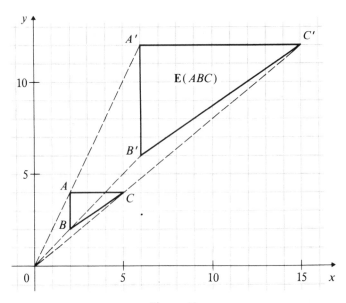

Figure 19

*11 When answering this question allow space on your diagram for values of x between $^-15$ and 20 and values of y between $^-10$ and 10.

Figure 20 shows a flag f and its image $\mathbf{E}(f)$ under $\mathbf{E}$, enlargement, centre $(3, 0)$ and scale factor $^-2$.

Let $\mathbf{T}$ be the translation with vector $\begin{bmatrix} ^-9 \\ 0 \end{bmatrix}$ and $\mathbf{D}$ be enlargement, centre $(7, 2)$ and scale factor 2.

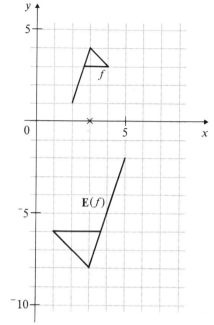

Figure 20

(a) Copy the diagram and add the flags $\mathbf{T}(f)$, $\mathbf{D}(f)$, $\mathbf{TE}(f)$ and $\mathbf{TD}(f)$.

(b) Describe the single transformations which map
   (i) f onto $\mathbf{TE}(f)$;
   (ii) f onto $\mathbf{TD}(f)$;
   (iii) $\mathbf{D}(f)$ onto $\mathbf{E}(f)$;
   (iv) $\mathbf{T}(f)$ onto $\mathbf{D}(f)$;
   (v) $\mathbf{D}(f)$ onto $\mathbf{T}(f)$;
   (vi) $\mathbf{TD}(f)$ onto $\mathbf{TE}(f)$.

12 Let $\mathbf{A}$ be reflection the line $x = 3$,
      $\mathbf{B}$ be reflection in the line $y = 1$,
      $\mathbf{H}$ be the rotation of $180°$ about $(0, 0)$
   and $\mathbf{Q}$ be the rotation of $^-90°$ about $(5, 0)$.
   If V is the point $(5, 6)$, what are the coordinates of:
      (a) $\mathbf{AA}(V)$;   (b) $\mathbf{BB}(V)$;   (c) $\mathbf{ABAB}(V)$;
      (d) $\mathbf{HH}(V)$;   (e) $\mathbf{AAAA}(V)$;   (f) $\mathbf{QQQQ}(V)$?

4. IDENTITY AND POWERS

The identity transformation

For a reflection $\mathbf{M}$, we notice that for any point P, $\mathbf{MM}(P) = P$, in other words doing $\mathbf{M}$ twice in succession is equivalent to doing nothing at all. We write $\mathbf{MM} = \mathbf{I}$, the identity transformation. $\mathbf{I}$ moves nothing; some call it the 'stay-put' transformation.

Index notation

We often write $\mathbf{M}^2$ for $\mathbf{MM}$ and $\mathbf{M}^3$ for $\mathbf{MMM}$. In this context index notation means that a transformation is to be repeated.

Exercise D

*1 Which of the following describe the identity transformation?
   (a) the translation $\begin{bmatrix} 0 \\ 0 \end{bmatrix}$;
   (b) the rotation of $360°$ about $(0, 0)$;

(c) the rotation of 360° about (2, 3);

(d) reflection in the x-axis;

(e) enlargement, centre (0, 0) and scale factor 1.

2   Let **X** be reflection in the x-axis,

Y be reflection in the y-axis,

and **H** be the half-turn (rotation of 180°) about (0, 0).

Referring to Figure 16, simplify

H($\Delta 4$),   **H**($\Delta 5$),   **H**($\Delta 6$),   **XY**($\Delta 4$),   **XY**($\Delta 5$),   **XY**($\Delta 6$).

Put into words the statement **XY = H**.

Simplify the following:

(a) **H**^{2} ;   (b) **YX**;   (c) **HX**;   (d) **XH**;   (e) **H**^{4} ;

(f) **X**^{2} ;   (g) **X**^{3} ;   (h) **XYXYXY**;   (i) **X**^{2}**Y**^{2}**H**^{2}.

*3   If **R** is *any* transformation and **I** is the identity transformation, what can you say about **RI**?

Simplify:

(a) **IR**;   (b) **RI**^{2};   (c) **IRIR**;   (d) **I**^{4}**R**^{4}.

4   If **L** and **M** are the translations with vectors $\begin{bmatrix} 4 \\ 5 \end{bmatrix}$ and $\begin{bmatrix} -3 \\ 6 \end{bmatrix}$, find the vectors for the trans-

lations **E**, **F** and **G** such that

(a) **LM = E**;   (b) **F = M**^{2} ;   (c) **EFG = I**.

*5   Let **S** denote the translation with vector $\begin{bmatrix} 2 \\ 3 \end{bmatrix}$ and **T** the translation with vector $\begin{bmatrix} -1 \\ 1 \end{bmatrix}$.

Write down the coordinates of the points onto which (0, 0) is mapped under the trans-

formations:

(a) **ST** ;   (b) **TS** ;   (c) **T**^{2} ;   (d) **S**^{3} ;

(e) **TS**^{2} ;   (f) **TST** ;   (g) **STS** ;   (h) **STST**.

6   **A** is the translation with vector $\begin{bmatrix} 3 \\ 4 \end{bmatrix}$ and **B** the translation with vector $\begin{bmatrix} -2 \\ 1 \end{bmatrix}$. If *P* is the

point ($^-$1, $^-$2), give the coordinates of the points:

(a) **A**(*P*);   (b) **B**(*P*);   (c) **AB**(*P*);   (d) **BA**(*P*) ;   (e) **B**^{3}**A**^{2}(*P*);

(f) **BABAB**(*P*).

5. COMBINATION OF REFLECTIONS

We have already had many examples in which one transformation followed by another is seen to be entirely equivalent to carrying out a single third transformation. We shall attempt a systematic treatment in a later chapter but we can make a start now by looking in detail at the combination of two reflections.

Exercise E

1   A piece of paper is folded three times, giving eight thicknesses altogether. The shaded parts (Figure 21 (b)) are then cut away. When the paper is unfolded, how many of the

(a)   (b)

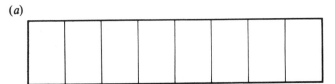

Figure 21

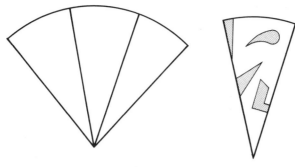

Figure 22

figures will be facing to the left? What will be the distance between two adjacent figures facing to the left?

2   Take a sector of a circle, fold it in three and cut out a pattern. (See Figure 22.) What does this show when unfolded?

3   Can you suggest from your experience so far what single transformation is equivalent to **CD** where **C** and **D** are reflections in two different lines c and d?

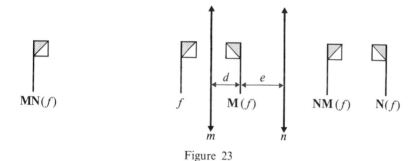

Figure 23

4   Figure 23 shows two parallel lines m and n. A flag f and four of its images have been labelled, where **M** and **N** are reflections in the lines m and n.
   (a) What single transformation **T** maps f onto **NM**(f)? Is there any connection between the distance needed to describe this transformation and the lengths d and e?
   (b) What happens if you apply this transformation **T** to **M** (f)? Why is **NM(M**(f)**)** or **NMM**(f) the same as **N**(f)?

*5 l is the line segment joining (3, 1) and (2, 4). If M_1 is reflection in the y-axis and M_2 is reflection in the line $x = 4$, find the coordinates of the endpoints of:
   (a) $M_1(l)$;   (b) $M_2(l)$;   (c) $M_1 M_2(l)$;   (d) $M_2 M_1(l)$.
   Describe the single transformations equivalent to $M_1 M_2$ and to $M_2 M_1$. How are these connected?

6   Draw two lines m and n with an angle of $60°$ between them and a simple figure f. Using tracing-paper, draw and label **M**(f), **N**(f), **MN**(f), **NM**(f), **MNM**(f) and **NMN**(f), where **M** and **N** are reflections in the lines m and n respectively. Describe the symmetries of the complete pattern.

7   Draw two lines p and q and a sword s as in Figure 24. Using tracing-paper, draw **P**(s) and **QP**(s), where **P** and **Q** are reflections in the lines p and q. What single transforma-

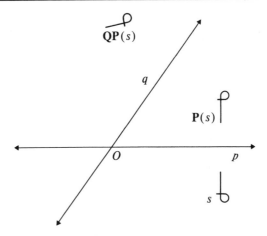

Figure 24

tion will map *s* onto **QP**(*s*)? To specify it precisely, you will need to measure an angle. What relation does this angle appear to have to the angle between *p* and *q*?

Draw **Q**(*s*) and **PQ**(*s*) as well and comment on the position of your final sword.

*8 Let **X** be reflection in the *x*-axis, **Y** be reflection in the *y*-axis and **A** be reflection in the line *y* = *x*. Describe the transformations:

(*a*) **YX**;   (*b*) **XY**;   (*c*) **YA**;   (*d*) **AX**;   (*e*) **AXAX**;   (*f*) **AXY**.

6. USE OF VECTORS

We have used vectors to describe translations. They can also be used to help find the images of points under other transformations.

Example 1

Find the image of *P* (8, 11) under enlargement with centre *A* (2, 7) and scale factor 2.

AP' is twice *AP* and *P'* is on the line *AP* so we can write $\underset{\sim}{AP'} = 2\underset{\sim}{AP}$. Now

$$\underset{\sim}{AP} = \begin{bmatrix} 6 \\ 4 \end{bmatrix}, \quad \text{so} \quad \underset{\sim}{AP'} = \begin{bmatrix} 12 \\ 8 \end{bmatrix}.$$

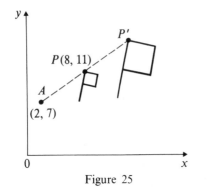

Figure 25

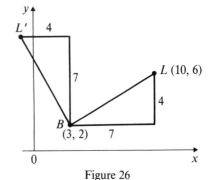

Figure 26

The translation with vector $\begin{bmatrix} 12 \\ 8 \end{bmatrix}$ takes A to P' so P' has coordinates $(2 + 12, 7 + 8) = (14, 15)$.

Example 2

Find the image of L (10, 6) under the rotation of 90° about B (3,2).

Figure 26 shows that $\underset{\sim}{BL} = \begin{bmatrix} 7 \\ 4 \end{bmatrix}$ and $\underset{\sim}{BL'} = \begin{bmatrix} ^-4 \\ 7 \end{bmatrix}$. L' therefore has coordinates $(3 + {}^-4, \quad 2 + 7) = ({}^-1, \ 9)$.

Exercise F

*1   Write down the vectors for the translations which map
  (a) (17, 48) onto (6, 83);   (b) (6, 83) onto (17, 48);
  (c) (22, 43) onto ($^-16$, 6);   (d) (2, 13) onto (27, 0).

2   Find the image of
  (a) (4, 1) under the translation with vector $\begin{bmatrix} 2 \\ 8 \end{bmatrix}$;
  (b) (19, 15) under the translation with vector $\begin{bmatrix} 12 \\ 30 \end{bmatrix}$.

*3   Find the images of (4, 1) under the rotations of 180° about
  (a) (0, 0);   (b) (7, 0);   (c) (9, 3);   (d) (4, 3).

4   (a) Copy Figure 27, allowing space for values of x between $^-20$ and 7 and y between $^-5$ and 7.
  (b) Find the centre (G) of the enlargement which maps one flower onto the other by finding where $D'D$ and $E'E$ meet when produced.
  (c) Write down the vectors $\underset{\sim}{GD}$, $\underset{\sim}{GD'}$, $\underset{\sim}{GE}$ and $\underset{\sim}{GE'}$.
  (d) What is the scale factor of the enlargement?

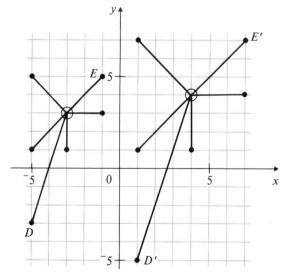

Figure 27

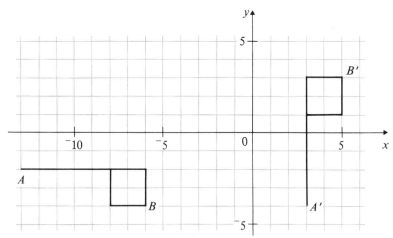

Figure 28

*5 Find the images of (4, 1) under enlargements with scale factor 3 and
  (a) centre (0, 0);   (b) centre (7, 0);   (c) centre (0, 8);   (d) centre (⁻16, ⁻9).

6 Copy Figure 28 and by drawing the mediators (perpendicular bisectors) of AA' and BB' find the centre C of the rotation which maps one flag onto the other. Write down the vectors $\underset{\sim}{C}A$, $\underset{\sim}{C}A'$, $\underset{\sim}{C}B$, and $\underset{\sim}{C}B'$.

*7 Find the images of (3, 8) under the rotations of 90° about:
  (a) (0, 0);   (b) (3, 0);   (c) (0, 6);   (d) (0, 8).

8 Find the images of (3, 8) under the rotations of ⁻90° about:
  (a) (0, 0);   (b) (3, 0);   (c) (0, 6);   (d) (0, 8).

SUMMARY

Transformations must be carefully specified, as follows:
Reflection: position of mirror line
Rotation: position of centre of rotation, angle of rotation
Translation: vector
Enlargement: position of centre of enlargement, scale factor

(Section 1)

An isometry is a transformation which leaves all lengths and angles unchanged. Rotation and translation are direct isometries – an object and its image are directly congruent. Reflection is an opposite isometry – an object and its image are oppositely congruent.   (Section 2)

$\mathbf{A}(f)$ denotes the image of a figure f under the transformation $\mathbf{A}$. $\mathbf{BA}(f)$ denotes the image of $\mathbf{A}(f)$ under the transformation $\mathbf{B}$.

A statement such as $\mathbf{AB} = \mathbf{C}$ means that the transformation $\mathbf{B}$ followed by $\mathbf{A}$ has the same effect as the single transformation $\mathbf{C}$ whatever object we choose.

$\mathbf{AB}$ is usually different from $\mathbf{BA}$.   (Section 3)

The identity transformation leaves every point of a figure unchanged. It is denoted by $\mathbf{I}$.

Index notation is used when a transformation is repeated, for example Q^3 means **QQQ**.   (Section 4)

Combination of reflections

If **M** is reflection in the line m, and **N** is reflection in the line n, then:

if m and n are parallel, **NM** is the translation through double the distance from m to n and perpendicular to m and n;

if m and n are intersecting lines, **NM** is the rotation about their point of intersection through double the angle from m to n.   (Section 5)

Summary exercise

1 Figure 29 shows a letter J and its images under various transformations. Describe precisely the single transformations **A**, **B**, **C**, **D** and **E**. (Hint for **C** and **D**; consider their effect on $A(j)$.)

2 In Figure 29, describe precisely the single transformations
   (*a*) equivalent to (i) **CA**;   (ii) **BA**;
   (*b*) which map (i) **DA**(j) to **BA**(j);   (ii) **BA**(j) to **CA**(j);   (iii) **BA**(j) to **E**(j).

3 If **T** is the translation with vector $\begin{bmatrix} -4 \\ -3 \end{bmatrix}$ and **R** is the rotation of $90°$ about the point (4, 3), draw a diagram to show **T**(j), **R**(j), **RT**(j) and **TR**(j) (where j is the letter J in Figure 29) and hence describe precisely the transformations equivalent to **RT** and **TR**.

4 Draw a letter L by joining the points (2, 6), (1, 2) and (4, 1).
   (*a*) Write down the single translation that will map it into the letter L joining $(^-3, 3)$, $(^-4, ^-1)$ and $(^-1, ^-2)$.
   (*b*) Write down the coordinates of the image of the first L under the translation with vector $\begin{bmatrix} 5 \\ 5 \end{bmatrix}$.
   (*c*) If the first letter L is translated so that (1, 2) maps onto (3, $^-2$), find the images of the other vertices.

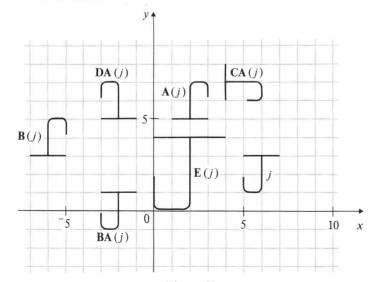

Figure 29

Miscellaneous exercise

1   Let **Q** denote the rotation of 240° about (⁻1, 2). Find the smallest value of z for which $\mathbf{Q}^z = \mathbf{I}$. What other values of z satisfy this equation?

2   What is the smallest value of n for which $\mathbf{A}^n = \mathbf{I}$ if **A** is a rotation through:
    (*a*) 40°;   (*b*) 60°;   (*c*) 80°;   (*d*) 100°?

3   Copy Figure 23 on a small scale and add the image flags **MNM**(f), **NMNM**(f) and **NMN**(f). Describe where **NMNMN**(f) and **MNMNMN**(f) would be. What is a simpler way of writing **MNNMNM**?

4   Copy Figure 30 and form an extended pattern by repeatedly rotating the motif through 180° about A and B alternately.

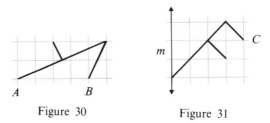

Figure 30   Figure 31

5   Form another freize pattern as in question 3 by copying Figure 31 and repeating alternately reflection in m and 180° rotation about C.

6   Look around your home, school and town for decorative repeating frieze patterns and compare their symmetries with ones you have produced.

7   A girl's face is about 30 cm from a mirror. In order to see the back of her hair she holds another mirror nearly parallel to the first, 20 cm behind her head. How far from her eyes does the back of her head appear to be? (Make a reasonable estimate for the dimensions of her head).

8   Draw a flag f whose shaft joins the points (2, 1) and (3, 4). Construct its image after reflections in the lines $y = 1$, $y = 2$, $y = 3$ and $y = 4$. What can you say about the set of images of a figure under a set of reflections in parallel lines?

9   Copy Figure 32. Let $\mathbf{M}_1$ denote reflection in the line m_1 and so on. Construct $\mathbf{M}_1(f)$ and $\mathbf{M}_2\mathbf{M}_1(f)$. Draw lines m'_1 and m'_2 parallel to m_1 and m_2 respectively. Construct $\mathbf{M}'_1(f)$ and $\mathbf{M}'_2\mathbf{M}'_1(f)$. How are $\mathbf{M}'_2\mathbf{M}'_1(f)$ and $\mathbf{M}_2\mathbf{M}_1(f)$ related? Discuss why you will obtain a similar result if you construct $\mathbf{M}_2\mathbf{M}'_1(f)$ and $\mathbf{M}'_2\mathbf{M}_1(f)$. State a general principle.

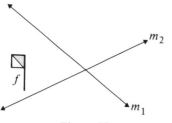

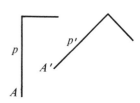

Figure 32   Figure 33

10 (a) In Figure 33 the figure p has been reflected in two straight lines v and w respectively and its image is p'. Do you think the lines v and w are parallel? Copy Figure 33 and construct the mirror-line v of the reflection which maps A onto A'. Construct also the image of p under this reflection and discuss how you can now reflect it onto the final position p'. Hence construct the line w. Are these the only possible positions for lines v and w? Use tracing-paper to construct the fixed point O of the rotation which maps p onto p'. What connection has O with v and w?

(b) Consider any convenient pair of directly congruent figures, A and B. Can A be mapped onto B by a single reflection? By a double reflection? (Consider the construction in part (a)). Does it make any difference if A and B are in parallel positions so that they can be related by a translation?

REVISION EXERCISE 8

1 Write as single fractions in their lowest terms:
   (a) $\frac{5}{4} - \frac{4}{5}$;   (b) $\frac{14}{15} \div \frac{10}{21}$;   (c) $2\frac{1}{2} \times \frac{3}{10}$;   (d) 4% of $7\frac{1}{2}$.

2 Write in standard form:
   (a) 0.000 230 5;   (b) $(4 \times 10^{-3}) \times (7 \times 10^{5})$;
   (c) $(7 \times 10^{5}) \div (4 \times 10^{-3})$;   (d) $(4.2 \times 10^{-3}) \div (7 \times 10^{5})$.

3 Write the following numbers (i) correct to three significant figures; (ii) correct to three decimal places:
   (a) 0.7405;   (b) 0.040 46;   (c) 60.4999;   (d) 0.002 508.

4 If $A = \{$prime factors of 1848$\}$ list the members of A and write down the value of $n(A)$.

5 Solve the following inequalities:
   (a) $3(x - 7) > 2x$;   (b) $2(5 - x) + 3 \leqslant 5x + 6$.

6 Make x the subject of the formula $p = q(b + x)$.

REVISION EXERCISE 9

1 Write down an expression for the total number of hours taken to travel p km at x km/h and q km at y km/h.

2 Solve the following equations for x:
   (a) $3(x - 7) = 55 + x$;   (b) $2.1(x - 3.7) = 5.03 + 1.3x$.

3 Mary runs three times as fast as she walks. Find her walking speed if by running for 15 minutes and walking for 40 minutes she travels a total distance of 6.8 km.

4 On January 1st 1921 the President of Ruritania awarded himself a 21% increase in his salary. His salary after the increase was 6 050 000 ruples a year.
   (a) What was his salary in 1920?
   (b) The constitution of Ruritania stipulates that the salary of the Grand Vizier shall be 32% of the President's salary. What was the Grand Vizier's salary in: (i) 1920; (ii) 1921?
   (c) What percentage increase in salary was the Grand Vizier awarded on 1 January 1921?

5 Describe the locus (in three dimensions) of the possible positions of Freda the fly, who flies within 20 cm of a light-bulb and within 30 cm of the ceiling if:
   (a) the light-bulb is 40 cm below the ceiling;
   (b) the light-bulb is 50 cm below the ceiling;
   (c) the light-bulb is 60 cm below the ceiling.

6 Make s the subject of the formula $v^2 = u^2 + 2as$.

REVISION EXERCISE 10

1 Estimate to an accuracy of one significant figure:
   (a) $0.0089 \times 909\ 000$;   (b) $0.0089 \div 909\ 000$.

2 If $f(x) = 1 - \frac{1}{4}x^2$ find:
   (a) $f(0)$;   (b) $f(\frac{1}{2})$;   (c) $f(\frac{2}{3})$;   (d) $f(2a)$.

3 Solve the following equation for z: $\dfrac{3}{2 + 5z} = 7$.

4 Draw a Venn diagram to illustrate the relation between three sets A, B and C for which $A \cap B = \varnothing$ and $C \subseteq B$.

5 A rectangle is measured and its length and width recorded as 5.7 cm and 4.6 cm. What is the smallest possible area of the rectangle?

6 The pressure at a depth h metres below the surface of a liquid of density ρ kg/m^3 is $h\rho g$ N/m^2 where g m/s^2 is the acceleration due to gravity. Taking $g = 9.81$, calculate the pressure at the bottom of a swimming-pool, 2.00 m below the surface, if the density of the (treated) water is 1005 kg/m^3.

7 Show in an accurate diagram the region $A \cap B$, where the regions A and B are given (using polar coordinates) as follows:
$$A = \{(r, t^\circ) : 3 < r < 5\}; \qquad B = \{(r, t^\circ) : 30 < t < 60\}.$$

8 Use a decimal search method to find, to an accuracy of three significant figures, a number y such that $y^5 = 27$.

Answers

Answers are given only to questions marked *, and when questions have parts (a), (b), (c) etc. answers are given to some of the parts only.

CHAPTER 1   FLOW CHARTS AND FUNCTIONS

Exercise B (p. 3)

1 $2 \longrightarrow 21 \longrightarrow 5 \longrightarrow 25 \longrightarrow 0.25$ (or $\frac{1}{4}$).

3 $\frac{1}{4} \longrightarrow \frac{3}{4} \longrightarrow {}^-\frac{1}{4} \longrightarrow {}^-1$.

5 $0.1 \longrightarrow 0.01 \longrightarrow 0.001$.

Exercise C (p.5)

1 (a) $f : x \longrightarrow 5x - 4$; $f(x) = 5x - 4$. (b) $f : x \longrightarrow 5(x - 4)$; $f(x) = 5(x - 4)$.

3 (a) (i) Start, Think of a number, Multiply by 3, Add 4, Stop;
     (ii) Start, Think of a number, Add 4, Multiply by 3, Stop.
   (b) $f(2) = 10$. (c) $g(2) = 18$.

Exercise D (p.8)

1 (a) $f(x) = x^2 + 3$; $f(2) = 7$. (b) $f(x) = (x + 3)^2$; $f(2) = 25$.

3 (a) $f(x) = \dfrac{1}{x} + 3$; $f(2) = 3\frac{1}{2}$. (b) $f(x) = \dfrac{1}{x + 3}$; $f(2) = \dfrac{1}{5}$.

5 (a) (i) Start, Think of a number, Square, Halve, Stop;
     (ii) Start, Think of a number, Halve, Square, Stop.
   (b) $f(6) = 18$; $g(6) = 9$.

7 (a) (i) Start, Think of a number, Change sign, Add 3, Stop;
     (ii) Start, Think of a number, Multiply by 3, Change sign, Add 1, Stop;
     or: Start, Think of a number, Change sign, Multiply by 3, Add 1, Stop;
     or: Start, Think of a number, Multiply by $^-3$, Add 1, Stop.
   (b) 3. (c) $\frac{1}{3}$.

9 (a) Start, Think of a number, Multiply by 3, Add 1, Square, Stop;
   (c) Start, Think of a number, Multiply by 4, Change sign, Add 3, Stop.

11 (a) $f(2) = 2$; $f(\frac{2}{3}) = \frac{2}{3}$.
   (b) $f : x \longrightarrow x$; $f(x) = x$.

Exercise E (p. 10)

1 $5, 2, {}^-1$.

3 $0, \frac{2}{3}, \frac{1}{2}$.

5 $f : x \longrightarrow x + 3$.

7 $f : x \longrightarrow 10 - x$.

9 $f : x \longrightarrow x^2$.

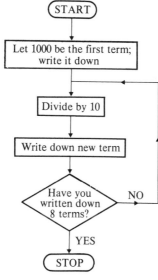

Figure A

Exercise F (p. 11)

1 (*a*) 1, 4, 7, 10, 13.

3 See Figure A; $t_6 = 0.01$; $t_8 = 0.0001$.

CHAPTER 2 STANDARD FORM

Exercise A (p. 18)

1 (*a*) 10^8 ;   (*c*) 10^2 ;   (*e*) 10^{-2} ;   (*g*) 10^{-5}.

2 (*a*) 10^2 ;   (*c*) 10^{-4} ;   (*e*) 10^2 ;   (*g*) 10^{-3}.

Exercise B (p. 19)

1 (*a*) 8×10^5 ;   (*c*) 4.82×10^4.

3 (*a*) 2800 ;   (*c*) 798 000.

5 (*a*) 1.5×10^8 km ;   (*c*) 2.99×10^8 m/s.

Exercise C (p. 20)

1 (*a*) 5.7×10^3 m ;   (*c*) 8.7×10^2 m ;   (*e*) 4.7×10^{-2} m.

2 (*a*) 1×10^{-2} m ;   (*c*) 2.3×10^{-1} m ;   (*e*) 3.63 m.

4 (*a*) 1×10^{-3} kg ;   (*c*) 3.17×10^{-2} kg ;   (*e*) 3.9×10^{-5} kg.

5 (*a*) 1×10^3 kg ;   (*c*) 2.5×10^5 kg.

6 (*a*) 10^6 ;   (*b*) (i) 4×10^6 m² ;   (iii) 5.6×10^{-4} m².

7 (*a*) (i) 5×10^4 m² ;   (iii) 3×10^3 m² ;   (*b*) (i) 1×10^{-4} ha ; (iii) 1×10^2 ha.

8 (*a*) (i) 5×10^{-3} m³ ;   (iii) 1×10^{-6} m³ ;   (*b*) (i) 10^3 l ;   (iii) 10^{-3} l ;
     (*c*) (i) 10^3 cm³ ;   (iii) 4×10^6 cm³.

Exercise D (p. 22)

1 6×10^7.   **3** 5×10^4.   **5** 2×10^{11}.

7 4.8×10^3.   **9** 3×10^{-4}.   **11** 4×10^2.

13 2.5×10^3.   **15** 4×10^{-7}.   **17** 5×10^1.
19 7.5×10^{-7}.

Exercise E (p. 23)
1 (a) £1000;   (c) 60 km/h.
3 (a) 200;   (c) 200;   (e) 0.02.
5 7×10^{54}.
7 2×10^7.

CHAPTER 3   USING A CALCULATOR

Exercise A (p. 29)

1 3.	**2** 10.	**3** 14.	**4** 6.	**5** $3\frac{1}{2}$.	**6** 10
7 6.	**8** 4.	**9** 10.	**10** 2.	**11** 6.	**12** $1\frac{1}{2}$.
13 13.	**14** 19.	**15** 25.	**16** 49.	**17** 8.	**18** 7.
19 4.	**20** 12.	**21** 36.	**22** 36.	**23** 3.	**24** 28.

Exercise B (p. 30)

1 0.5.	**2** 0.1.	**3** 0.1$\dot{6}$.	**4** 1.	**5** 0.8$\dot{3}$.	**6** 0.8$\dot{3}$.
7 0.$\dot{3}$.	**8** 1.	**9** 1.	**10** 1.	**11** 0.$\dot{7}$.	**12** 3.
13 0.5.	**14** 2.	**15** 3.			

Exercise C (p. 30)

1 $^-$1.	**2** 3.	**3** $^-$5.	**4** 1.	**5** $^-$6.
6 $^-$6.	**7** 6.	**8** $^-$3.	**9** 3.	**10** 9.

Exercise D (p. 31)
1 (a) 9.2;   (c) 24.244;   (e) 26.97;
(g) 16.32;   (i) 12.65;   (k) 12.
2 (a) 26.21;   (c) 56.01;   (e) $^-$14.26;
(g) 161.29;   (i) 2.25;   (k) 45.414.
5 £347.35.
7 £5.76.

Exercise E (p.33)
1 (a) 8;   (c) 13;   (e) 200;   (g) 0.2.
2 (a) 800;   (c) 9×10^5;   (e) 0.08;   (g) 5×10^{-4}.
3 (a) 17.3;   (c) 1.73×10^4;   (e) 0.548;   (g) 5.48×10^{-4}.

Exercise F (p. 34)
1 (a) 2.65;   (c) 2.71.

Exercise G (p. 37)

1 147.3516.	**3** 229.908.	**5** 0.042 81.
7 6.5363.	**9** 323.9448.	**11** 0.394 029 9
13 0.028 09 (to 4 s.f.).	**15** 0.051 47 (to 4 s.f.).	**17** 0.050 243 409.
19 $^-$0.875 865 (to 6 s.f.).	**21** $^-$0.648.	**23** 0.007 561 (to 4 s.f.).

CHAPTER 4 THE LANGUAGE OF ALGEBRA

Exercise A (p. 41)

1 (a) 45 pence;   (b) 60 pence;   (c) $15n$ pence.
3 (a) $5x$ pence;   (b) $15x$ pence;   (c) qx pence.
5 (a) 43 cm;   (b) $(x + 20)$ cm;   (c) $(3x + y)$ cm.
7 (a) 96 cm^2;   (b) $4q$ cm^2;   (c) lw cm^2.
9 (a) 10;   (b) 50;   (c) $\dfrac{n}{3}$.

Exercise B (p. 42)

1 (a) 5;   (c) 20.   **3** (a) 13;   (c) 25.
5 (a) 21 cm^2;   (c) 30 cm^2.   **7** (a) 16 km;   (c) 64 km.
9 (a) 6×10^{-3} mm.

Exercise C (p. 44)

1 (a) $7a$;   (c) $2c$.   **3** (a) $2p + 6$;   (c) $7r + s$.
5 (a) a;   (c) $\frac{5}{2}c$.   **7** (a) $2a + 6$;   (c) c.
9 (a) $3a - 21$;   (c) $3c - 1$.   **11** (a) $10a$;   (c) $12c$.

Exercise D (p. 46)

1 (a) $14q^2$;   (c) $12p^3$.   **3** (a) $2p^2q$;   (c) $20r^2 s^2$.
5 (a) $4m$;   (c) 1.   **7** (a) $4x^3$;   (c) $\frac{2}{3}a$.
9 (a) $6a^2$;   (c) $6c^2$.   **11** (a) $60x$ cm^2;   (b) $24q^2$ cm^3;   (c) $60t^3$ cm^3.

Exercise E (p. 48)

1 $7q = 63$.   **3** $a + b + 6 = 20$.
5 $60t \geqslant 200$.   **7** $7x + 9y = 340$.   **9** $60t > 50(t + 1)$.

CHAPTER 5 SETS

Exercise A (p. 57)

2 (a) The set of cards of children who live more than 4 km away from school or who travel to school by bus.
4 (a) $B \cup D$.
6 (a) $\{a, b, c, d, e, f, g, h, i, j, k, l, m, n, o\}$.
8 (a) The cards of children who live 4 km or less from the school.
10 (a) True.

Exercise B (p. 59)

1 (a) See Figure A.
3 See Figure B.
5 $n(C) = 4$, $n(B) = 5$, $n(A) = 7$, $n(D) = 13$.
7 (a) 15.
9 See Figure C.

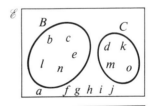

Figure A

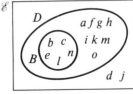

Figure B

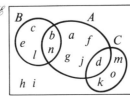

Figure C

Exercise C (p. 60)

1 See Figure D.

3 See Figure E.

5 See Figure F.

7 See Figure G.

9 $Y = \{1, 2, 3, 4\}$; $Z = \{2, 3\}$.

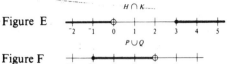

Figure D

Figure E

Figure F

Figure G

CHAPTER 6 LOCI

Exercise A (p. 65)

1 See Figure A, in which the possible positions are in the shaded region.

3 (*a*) A straight line.

5 See Figure B.

9 4 cm ; see Figure C.

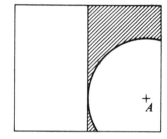

Figure A

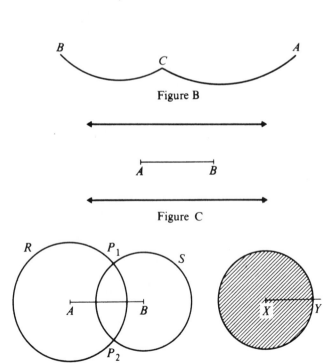

Figure B

Figure C

Figure D

Figure E

Exercise B (p. 69)

1 (c) $\{P : PB = PC\}$.

3 See Figure D; $R \cap S = \{P_1, P_2\}$.

5 See Figure E;   no.

Exercise C (p. 71)

1 See Figure F;   (a) (5, 2);   (b) $A \cap C = \emptyset$.

3 See Figure G.   **5** See Figure H.

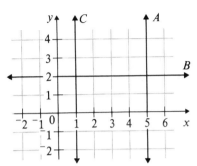

Figure F

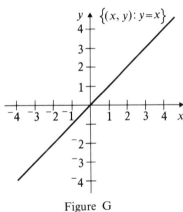

$\{(x, y) : y = x\}$

Figure G

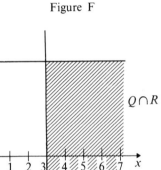

$Q \cap R$

Figure H

7 (a) See Figure I;   (c) See figure J.

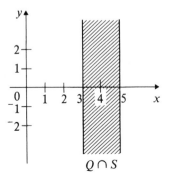

$Q \cap S$

Figure I

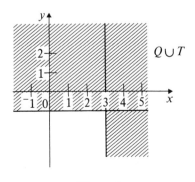

$Q \cup T$

Figure J

9   See Figure K.   **11**   See Figure L.

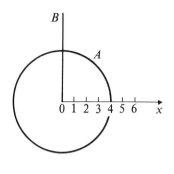

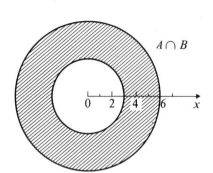

Figure K   Figure L

13   See Figure M.
15 $\{(r, t^\circ): r > 3 \text{ and } 0 < t < 90\}$.

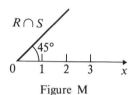

Figure M

Exercise D (p. 74)

1   Locus of *B* : part of a circle centre *A*, radius *AB* ; locus of *F* : part of a circle of the same radius.

3   *M* and *N* meet ; *T* and *U* move along the mediator of *AB*.

7   Scale factor $= \dfrac{AF}{AE} = \dfrac{AC}{AB}$.

Exercise E (p. 77)

5   (*a*) (i) $FA = FB$;   (ii) $FB = FC$.
        (*c*) *F* is on the mediator of *AC*.
9   See Figure N ; *AP* is the bisector of angle *BAC*.

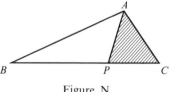

Figure N

Exercise F (p. 80)

1   (*a*) The surface of a hemisphere of radius 30 m.
3   (*a*) The surface of a cylinder whose axis is *l* and of radius 3m.
5 $\{P : PN < PS\}$ where *N* is the North Pole and *S* the South Pole.
7   The two planes bisecting the angles between the lines and perpendicular to the plane containing the lines.

CHAPTER 7   EQUATIONS

Exercise A (p. 84)

1   (*a*) 4.   **3**   (*a*) \$47.   **5**   (*a*) $a = 3$;   (*c*) $c = 8$.
7   (*a*) $w = 3\frac{1}{2}$;   (*c*) $y = 3.2$.   **9**   (*a*) 3.   **11**   (*a*) $p = 2\frac{1}{2}$;   (*c*) $r = 11$.

Exercise B (p. 87)

1 (a) $x = 7$. **3** (a) $z = 3$. **5** (a) $m = 5$. **7** (a) $z = 2$. **9** (a) $w = 7$.

Exercise C (p. 88)

1 (a) $x = 3$; (c) $a = {}^-2$.

3 (a) $x = 2$; (c) $u = 3$.

Exercise D (p. 89)

1 (a) (i) $n - 200$; (iii) $80(n - 200)$ pence; (b) $140n - 16\,000 = 68\,000$, $n = 600$; (c) 1000.

3 (a) (i) $\dfrac{5z}{60}$; (iii) $\dfrac{10(63 - z)}{60}$; (c) $3.5\,\text{km}$.

5 6p. **7** 12 kg.

Exercise E (p. 90)

1 See Figure A. (a) True; (c) False.

3 (a) $4, 5, 100$; (c) $4, 5, 100$.

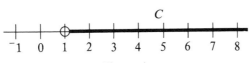

Figure A

Exercise F (p. 91)

1 $x > 4$. **3** $x \leqslant 7$. **5** $x > {}^-6$. **7** $x < 5$. **9** $x > 7$.

Exercise G (p. 92)

1 (a) $t = 1.5$; (c) (i) $t = 2.5$.

3 (a) $R = 55$; (c) (i) 20 ohms; (iii) 180 ohms.

5 (a) 24 seconds; (c) (i) 72 seconds.

7 (a) $x = \dfrac{y + 2}{3}$; (c) $x = \dfrac{v - b}{a}$; (e) $x = \dfrac{a}{t} - a$.

CHAPTER 8 RATIO AND PERCENTAGE

Exercise A (p. 98)

1 (a) $1 : 14$ (c) $1 : 7$ (e) $1 : 0.03$

3 (a) $1 : 81.2$

5 (a) £3 and £2.40.

7 (a) 80, 120 and 160.

9 0.888 kg.

Exercise B (p. 99)

1 (a) 25%; (c) 44%.

3 (a) $\frac{1}{5}$; (c) $\frac{1}{8}$.

5 (a) 5% of £24 = 0.05 × £24 = £1.20.
  (c) 49% of 16 447 votes = 0.49 × 16 447 votes = 8059 votes.

7 (a) 9%;   (c) 32.5%.

9 $£\dfrac{6x}{100} = £\dfrac{3x}{50}$.

Exercise C (p. 101)

1 £18.20.   **3** 111 754.   **5** £45.54.   **7** DM 8.81.   **9** £6.86.
11 123.30 fr.   **13** 76 074.   **15** 42 cm².   **17** 16%.
19 (a) 9.4%;   (c) 10.73%.

Exercise D (p. 102)

1 32%.   **3** 31.25%.   **5** 125%.   **7** 135.2637%.   **9** 2.80 m.

Exercise E (p. 104)

1 (a) 0.92;   (c) 0.75.   **3** £19.55.   **5** 30.83 m.   **7** 10.63%.   **9** 23.2%.
11 564 pupils.   **13** 40 000 rabbits.   **15** (a) £14 250;   (b) $33\frac{1}{3}$%.   **17** 17 days.

CHAPTER 9 ACCURACY

Exercise A (p. 109)

3 (a) 13.65 m ≤ length < 13.75 m;   (c) 13.695 m ≤ length < 13.705 m.
5 (a) 2999.5 m/s ≤ speed < 3000.5 m/s;   (c) 79.5°C ≤ temperature < 80.5°C.

Exercise B (p. 112)

1 (a) 3.5 m;   (b) 3.6975 m, 3.3075 m;   (c) No; 3.5 ± 0.2 m.
3 (a) 19 × 19 × 14 = 5054.
5 (a) 612 m³;   (c) 1.
7 (a) 8.85 m/s.
9 (a) 220 minutes.

CHAPTER 10 TRANSFORMATIONS

Exercise B (p. 121)

1 (a) The rotation of 180° about (0, 0).
3 (a) No: an opposite isometry will be required.
5 The rotation of 180° about (5, ⁻3) followed by the rotation of 180° about (0, 0).
7 Yes: the rotation of 180° about $(2, 3\frac{1}{2})$.
9 Reflection in the line $y = {}^-x$.

Exercise C (p. 124)

1 (a) True;   (c) False: $C(\Delta 5) = \Delta 2$ or $C(\Delta 6) = \Delta 1$.
3 (a) $X(\Delta 4) = \Delta 5$;   (c) $YB(\Delta 7) = \Delta 5$.
5 (a) False: $AA(\Delta 2) = \Delta 2$ or $AA(\Delta 8) = \Delta 8$;   (c) True.
8 (a) The rotation of 180° about (4, 3);   (c) the translation with vector $\begin{bmatrix} -8 \\ 6 \end{bmatrix}$.

11   (*b*) (i) Enlargement, centre $(0, 0)$ and scale factor $^-2$;
(iv) enlargement, centre $(^-11, 2)$ and scale factor 2.

Exercise D (p. 127)

1   All except (*d*).

3   (*a*) **R**;   (*c*) **R**^{2}.

5   (*a*) $(1, 4)$;   (*c*) $(^-2, 2)$;   (*e*) $(3, 7)$;   (*g*) $(3, 7)$.

Exercise E (p. 128)

5   (*a*) $(^-3, 1)$ and $(^-2, 4)$;   (*c*) $(^-5, 1)$ and $(^-6, 4)$.

8   (*a*) The rotation of $180°$ about the origin;   (*c*) the rotation of $90°$ about the origin;
(*e*) the rotation of $180°$ about the origin.

Exercise F (p. 131)

1   (*a*) $\begin{bmatrix} ^-11 \\ 35 \end{bmatrix}$;   (*c*) $\begin{bmatrix} ^-38 \\ ^-37 \end{bmatrix}$.   **3**   (*a*) $(^-4, ^-1)$;   (*c*) $(14, 5)$.

5   (*a*) $(12, 3)$;   (*c*) $(12, ^-13)$.   **7**   (*a*) $(^-8, 3)$;   (*c*) $(^-2, 9)$.

Index

150   Index